TO TREVOR

GOD BLESS

BILL & SHARON

twenty-five words

How the
Serenity Prayer
Can Save
Your Life

twenty-five words

Barb Rogers

Conari Press

First published in 2005 by
Red Wheel/Weiser, LLC
With offces at:
500 Third Street, Suite 230
San Francisco, CA 94107
www.redwheelweiser.com

ISBN: 978-1-59003-072-1

Library of Congress Cataloging-in-Publication Data

Rogers, Barb
    twenty-five words : how the Serenity prayer can save your life/
    Barb Rogers.
        p. cm.
    ISBN 1-59003-072-9
    1. Serenity prayer. I. Title.
BV284.S47R64 2005   2004025357
242'.7—dc22
Typeset in HoeflerText

Printed in Canada
TCP
10 9 8 7 6 5

I DEDICATE THIS BOOK,
in loving memory, to those women who helped
to shape my life, loved and supported me.
They will live in my heart forever:

My mother, Charline Chaplin
My stepmother, Connie Chaplin
My aunts, Ruth Poffinbarger, Juanita Kibler,
Fern Brannon, Ellen McMillan, and Genevieve Osborne
My sisters-in-law, Roberta Doty and Marcella Rodgers
My friends, Neeva Greeson, Marge DeHollander,
and Helen Wright

And in memory of the fur people who loved me in spite of
myself with a loyalty not to be compared: Pedro, Spike,
Junior, Domino, Teddy, and my sweet Angel who got me
through so much. My brother's companions, Sonny and
Essie Mae, Dad's Tina, and my friend Donna's Maxie. How
blessed I was to have them as part of my life.

And to Greg Robinson, whom we lost last year. You will be
missed, but your memory will live on.

Contents

Contents

Acknowledgments

...xru to so many people in my life for their love
...r. My brother, Bill, and my father, Charlie
...nd his wife, Florence. And to the Rogers family,
...so many to name. I am so honored to have been a
part of your family. And to Travis Hughes, my stepson and
a wonderful friend.

And to my gal pals ... what would I do without you girls in
my life? Thanks for everything:

Tammi Clancy
Jacqui McKibben
Cheryl Robinson
Donna Gordon & Nikki
Ruth Belden
Susan Miller
Regina Juarez
Cindy Daly
Marie Reid
Elva Adams
Karla Backlund
Maree Gurerson

Acknowledgments

I AM THANKFUL to so many people in my life for their love and support. My brother, Bill, and my father, Charlie Chaplin, and his wife, Florence. And to the Rogers family, who are too many to name. I am so honored to have been a part of your family. And to Travis Hughes, my stepson and a wonderful friend.

And to my gal pals . . . what would I do without you girls in my life? Thanks for everything:

Tammi Clancy
Jacqui McKibben
Cheryl Robinson
Donna Gordon & Nikki
Ruth Belden
Susan Miller
Regina Juárez
Cindy Daly
Marie Reid
Elva Adams
Karla Backlund
Maree Gutterson

Chassie West
Phoebe Bitner
Catherine Tarelton
Elaine Flinn
Gemma Lizada
Jem Hopkins
Dr. Laura Pasten
Sharon Bestwick
Nancy Walker from the Cornerstone Bakery
Shelly Burgerson, Donelle Lofton, and Anna Bennett
from the Ranch House Restaurant
And, special thanks to the Highland family. You are a
part of everything I do.

And always to my husband, Jr., and our two fur babies,
Sammi and Georgie, who complete my life and make
everything worthwhile. All my love and thanks.

THE SERENITY PRAYER

God, grant me the serenity
to accept the things I cannot change,
courage to change the things I can,
and wisdom to know the difference.

—Attributed to Reinhold Niebuhr

The Serenity Prayer

THE SERENITY PRAYER speaks to us of change. From the point of conception, life is change, whether we like it or not. We may not have control over many of the changes that take place in our lives, but there comes a time when we must decide whether to allow our circumstances and other people to dictate our lives, or to become coauthors of our destiny.

Two people get together to make us into a human being. Genetically, that may determine what we look like, predispose us to certain things, but we are *not* our parents. They are simply the vessels that created our body. The very essence of who we are comes from somewhere else. From the moment we draw our first breath, we embark on an experience that can only be ours, totally unique.

Early on, significant others will attempt to guide us with their truths, those things they have learned through their life experiences. At some point, we are all faced with a choice. We can accept their truth as our own, or we can have the courage to say, to ourselves and them, "This is my truth. . . . This is what I believe." And what we truly believe is our truth will shape our world.

As we age, live through many life experiences and choices, some better than others, what we believe will go through many changes. Where we are at the moment, what we have learned, what we have experienced, is the only truth we can live. That's not to say we can't be open and willing to change.

Have you ever sat glued to your television, totally in awe of the story of someone who has overcome great odds? Did you wonder what you would have done given the same set of circumstances? Even though you may not be happy with your own life, did you think you should be grateful because it wasn't as bad as the person's in the story? When you think that way—compare yourself to others—you are cheating yourself. Just like the person in the story, you have been given a set of circumstances to deal with. They are yours alone. You can't understand the person in the story any more than they can understand you. The best you can do is accept that that is the life they were given, for whatever reason, and focus on the life you were given, the choices you are making.

Each individual has their own questions about life, about the purpose for their existence, the meaning of it all. There are those who would allow others to influence their answers to life. There are those who believe there are no answers, so why bother? And there are seekers. The seekers are the ones who will become coauthors of their lives. They are the ones who will live life to the fullest, understand a need to experience all emotion, stay open to the truth of who they are, and embrace the gifts of choice and change.

At age thirty-five, after a life filled with unhappiness, struggle to survive, and frustration, I made the choice to become a seeker. I've heard it said that when the student is ready, the teacher appears. Although I'm certain I'd seen the Serenity Prayer many times before—on cards, laminated onto a plaque, embroidered on a wall hanging—I didn't understand it. The prayer was simply words, pretty words and a nice thought, until my life brought me to the point of need—to the point of becoming a seeker, to the point of understanding there had to be a better way.

It was such a simple little prayer, those few lines that said so much and gave me hope. Serenity, peace, seemed so far away. Considering how my life had gone, if I could just find a bit of it, I would have felt overpaid. But it gave me so much more. If I could have planned out my life, it couldn't be better than it is today. I would have sold myself short. The Serenity Prayer was the beginning of a fulfilled life: a life filled with love, laughter, and a happiness I never knew existed. The prayer gave me freedom from the past, from the expectation of others, from the dread of each new day. Today, I look forward to every moment, to every new sunrise, with the anticipation of a child experiencing everything for the first time.

Life is not going to just happen to me. I am not going to make it happen. My life is going to be a happening on a daily basis. Through the grace of a God of my understanding and truly living the words of the Serenity Prayer, I have found my truth for today.

If you have become a seeker, have decided to take part in your life, to accept the gifts of choice and change, perhaps, like me, this wonderful prayer can be an inspiration. Ask yourself the hard questions. Be honest with yourself. Who are you? What do you believe? Does what you believe make you happy? Do you know serenity? Are you living or just going through the motions? If you can't answer these questions, or aren't satisfied with your answers, and I told you there was a better way to live, would you be willing to take the risk? If your life is unhappy, unfulfilled, if you dread each new day, what have you got to lose?

By truly understanding the Serenity Prayer, putting the words into action, I can guarantee you will be happy, joyous, and free. I know this because I am living proof and because I've seen it happen in the lives of others. Many of us, including me, were broken people, people for whom others would have said there was no hope. I was the child you wouldn't want your children to play with, the girl that mothers feared for their sons, the wife from hell, the mother who didn't have a clue, the person you would avoid on the street, at a social function, certainly not someone you would want as a friend. Not so today.

Today, my life is filled with friends, love, laughter, a life that exceeded all expectations. What changed? I did—with help from a God of my understanding and the Serenity Prayer lived out on a daily basis. It takes God, acceptance, courage, and wisdom.

God, Grant Me the Serenity

NO ONE CAN PROVE to me there is no God, any more than I can prove to them there is a God. We all are brought to that belief through our own life experiences. Some of us are born into a specific religion, raised to believe certain things; others encounter the question of God at some point in their lives. But no matter how we come to the choice, it is a personal matter that no one else can decide for us.

Many years ago, I heard a speaker whose story had great impact on me. From the beginning of his life, he was raised by his mother and grandmother to be a priest. His young life was spent in training, in church, in prayer, in learning what was expected of him. And he became a priest. The problem was, he didn't believe in God. Yes, he knew the right words to say, knew how to teach others, was fulfilling the expectations of others, but inside lived an unhappy, frustrated person plagued by questions.

As with most unhappy human beings, he began to act out his true feelings. He nearly lost everything and everyone in his life before he came to a God of his understanding, until he found a true faith that all the words of others could not give him.

Like the priest, I was given messages by others. I was a waste, a little heathen who would never amount to anything. God was the first half of a swear word. If he was out there, up there, or wherever, he sure wouldn't waste a minute's notice on someone like me . . . except to punish me. That's what I believed, so it became my reality . . . the world I lived in. Everything bad that happened was God's fault, and the few good things in my life were directly related to me. Even when something good happened, I couldn't enjoy it because I always wondered when the other shoe would drop.

I will probably never forget my first real encounter with the Serenity Prayer. It was at a low point in my life. I walked into a twelve-step meeting. There it was, in bold, black letters, on the wall behind the chairperson. They started the meeting by reciting it in unison. Not me. I wasn't speaking to God. I wasn't asking him for anything. As far as I could see, he'd already given me more than I could stand. Otherwise, why would I be there in that place, with a bunch of strangers, sick, scared, and shaking?

The first line of the prayer put me off. Even as time passed, my health improved; I could think more clearly; I couldn't get passed that first line: "God, grant me the serenity."

My mind screamed, "All he ever gave me was misery." At that point, I'd lived through abuse, rape, the death of my children, many disastrous relationships, a mental hospital, and addiction. I had nothing, and there was no one left who cared if I stepped off the face of the Earth.

Determined as I was to find a better way to live, I formed a plan. I would become a minimalist, not own anything that I cared about, stay away from real involvement and feelings with other people, and use all the wisdom and knowledge I could gather that didn't involve God. I know it sounds crazy now, but at the time, it made sense to me. If I didn't have anything, no one could take it from me. If I didn't love anyone, I wouldn't get hurt. If I ignored God, maybe he would leave me alone.

Not having possessions wasn't difficult. I'd lost everything. I moved into a half of a garage, minimally furnished, and started my new life. It took money to live, even though I was living poorly. I needed a job. Since I wasn't well thought of in the small town where I lived—and the residents had good reason—the job search did not go well. When I was nearly out of money and food and wondered how I would keep a roof over my head, I went to a person I'd met in one of the meetings. I poured out my story of woe. He said, "Have you prayed about it?"

I fought back the tears. He didn't understand. No one understood. I'd prayed when my babies were sick. They died. I prayed when my mother shot herself. She died. I prayed when my oldest son got in trouble. He died. Every time I fell into a traumatic situation, I'd told God what to do, but he never heard me. I wouldn't ask him for another thing.

Today, I'm sure that man must have seen the pain in my eyes because he said, "This time, why don't you ask God what his will for you is—to put you where you need to be?"

As I walked home, his words haunted my mind. For several days, I questioned, agonized, tortured myself with memories of past prayers. Desperate times call for desperate measures. I had to do something, and I didn't have much left to lose. I prayed, and I did it the way he said.

Little did I know, that day was the beginning of my new life. Through a set of strange circumstances, a job was put in my path. It wasn't the type of work I would have sought out; I had no experience in the field. It barely paid enough for me to get by, but it ended up being one of the best things that ever happened to me.

I would be a daily caregiver for an older, ill lady, who had to have 'round-the-clock care. I told this woman and her family the truth about myself because I knew someone in that small town would. They hired me anyway. I spent my days with this fine lady, this woman whom I came to love, in spite of my plan. She had lived through her own tragedies, had faced the illnesses that were racking her body—but she knew God—had an unwavering faith that I had never known.

She was the epitome of living the Serenity Prayer. And in my time with her, I began to understand what the words meant. Through seeing how she lived on a daily basis, listening to her, I realized that the rest of the Serenity Prayer meant nothing until I could find a way to a God of my understanding, a faith to ignite hope, a willingness to risk living again. I realized I was simply existing, and I had a choice. I could stay with the plan, in a life that was safe but meant nothing, or take the risk. Go out on a limb and ask God to show me the way . . . his way.

One of the problems with turning things over to a God of our choosing is that we are no longer in charge, and may have trouble giving up control. Truth was, for me at least, when I was left to my own devices, in control, I made a real mess of it. How much worse could it have gotten? I became a seeker. I talked to others, people like the woman I cared for, people who had found a better way, read books about spirituality, but still, there was that part of me that didn't want to give in, to surrender to the unknown.

One lady told me to tape three prayers to my bathroom mirror. Each morning, I was to read them aloud. I began doing that. Another person said that at night to give thanks for three things. I did that. It became my habit to read the Serenity Prayer, the Lord's Prayer, and the Universal Prayer aloud. When I lay my head on my pillow, I thanked God for three things, even if it was simply enough to eat, a place of shelter, and the ability to walk to work. Through those acts, I began to feel better, but in me there was always something missing. I never really felt that connection to God.

Have you ever had that feeling? It's like being in a room full of people and feeling totally alone. It's about not fitting in anywhere, always on the outside looking in. I watched people, listened to them speak of their lives, saw what they had, but couldn't figure out how they got there. Somehow, I always knew I would never be allowed to know the secret handshake that would allow me to join the club called humanity. What I didn't know was I was about to embark on a life lesson that would open all the doors to me.

My special lady, whom I'd allowed myself to love, was near her time to cross over. I knew time was short. The death of a loved one was my trigger to self-destruct. I began to prime myself for the inevitable. I could not lose anyone else. Why had I allowed myself to care?

When the moment of choice was at hand, instead of running away, instead of self-destructing, I listened to a voice. It wasn't the voice of God. . . . Well, maybe, if he was talking through another human being. A man once said to me, "The time will come when you will get on your knees and truly believe." I heard that voice in my mind.

I dropped to my knees in the open doorway and truly asked for help . . . begged for help. God swooped me up in his strong, safe arms, and I knew, from that moment on, everything would be okay. I figured out that the secret handshake is surrender, and the door stays open as long as I stay connected on a daily basis. The connection is through prayer. Today, I am never alone, and I fit in anywhere God chooses for me to be.

The serenity is in a sense of knowing. It's not like thinking things will be okay. It's *knowing it* within the deepest part of our being. All doubts, all fears are removed; the missing part is there; the part that has been broken is healed.

It may have taken me a long time and a lot of misery to get to the point of surrender, but once there, the result was instantaneous. Once there, I understood that this is what I'd been moving toward my entire life. It took me every moment, every experience, every person I'd encountered, to bring me to that one moment on my knees. I knew there was a plan, and I was a part of it. My life was forever changed.

It had always seemed to me that the first line of the Serenity Prayer should have been at the bottom, that through acceptance, courage, and wisdom, we would know serenity. I now know whoever wrote it had it right. Without knowing a God of our understanding, the acceptance, courage, and wisdom will elude us. God's gift of serenity is the knowing that all these things are possible.

Are you thinking, "This all sounds real nice, but how does it work in real life?" It's a big commitment. Will I have to don my best clothes, attend church, donate money, go out and find people to help? What about fun? Do I get to have fun anymore? Do I really want to be that nice? Will I have to run around witnessing to the world about God? I don't know if I can do it . . . or want to do it.

It's normal to have doubts, questions about what life will be like, what changes will take place once we make that connection to a God of our understanding. I had plenty of them. For one thing, I wondered what was meant by a God of my understanding. I barely understood what it was to be human.

I was not raised in religion, but once, when I was young, I attended Sunday School and church twice a week. My mother, who was alcoholic and drug addicted, was told she had an incurable lung disease. I guess she figured it was time to get religious. Of course, her idea of religion was to drink vodka because someone said no one could smell it. Between that and the pills, it made for an interesting experience.

She chose a local church whose teachings included not going to movies, girls not wearing pants, or jewelry or cutting their hair. They spoke of a big, mean God who swooped down and wiped out entire groups of people. Even as a child, I questioned what I was being taught. I wondered why some God who was supposed to be in charge of the whole world cared whether I wore a dress or not. He surely had bigger concerns.

But there I was, and as long as she decided we would be involved, I had no choice. That might help you understand that later, when my children died, it wasn't a stretch for me to believe God was a baby killer and that I was surely being punished for some untoward deed or thought I'd had. And there were plenty of them to pick from.

The religious experience was cut short due to unforeseen circumstances. I'll leave that to your imagination. The point is, although I didn't believe much of what I was told, it instilled doubts in my mind, questions about why anyone would want to devote themselves to that God. I didn't understand that I got to choose . . . to decide what I believed and what I believed God to be.

It was suggested to me, if I felt the need, that I picture a God in human form. He could look any way I chose. I found that in my mind, he looked a lot like Santa Clause, but without the red suit. What can I say? It worked for me. It wasn't just about the look, but the demeanor. I liked the idea of that twinkle in his eye, a sense of humor and a hearty laugh, of fairness, the love of children, and his endless ability to give and to know what we need even before we do. It seemed like the perfect choice to me. I just wanted to snuggle into his big arms, be held close, and know that no matter what, he would love me. That's how I came to know a God of my understanding.

With this picture in my heart, as I entered real life each day, simply as a matter of course things looked better. Because I was no longer alone, as my faith grew, the fear subsided, and I felt better and better about who I was; it became easier to make choices that enhanced my life instead of destroying it.

I did not have to dress to please this God of my understanding. I did not have to go into a specific building to feel him with me. I did not have to go out and find people who needed help. They seemed to wander into my line of vision. All I had to do was to see the opportunities when they presented themselves.

What I found to be true, for myself, is I don't have to be anything more than I am. After all, if he made me in his image, how bad can I be? It is more important to understand the truth of who I am and live in that truth than to attempt to put myself into an image that I think God and the world want me to be. So, I get to be who I am, fully and completely. How great is that?

Fun? I can tell you I am one of the happiest people I know. I get high on air. I find joy in the smallest things. I am living more fully today than I ever thought possible. I don't have to go out and tell people about God . . . not unless they ask. The best witness I can be is to live well and be happy, to attempt to emulate what I believe God to be.

ated. If we want God, and others, to be kind, forgiving, loving, with a wonderful sense of humor; if we want to feel safe and accepted in his presence, then that is what we should be for ourselves, for those who enter our life. After all, how can we ask God to forgive us, ask others to forgive us, and not forgive ourselves? How can we ask God to grant us serenity, then deny ourselves the very thing we most desire?

Quite simply, once we make that connection to a God of our understanding, we are worthy just because *we are*. What we need to understand is that who we are is what matters, not what we accomplish or attain in life. Think about it. When we leave here, the only thing we are taking with us is us. There will be no house to hide in, no car to run away in, no clothes to disguise who we are. The masks will be torn away. We will stand in truth.

Be careful when you paint that picture of God in your mind. Whatever it is we expect of our creation, we should be willing to give ourselves. So, once we establish what we believe to be true, the time to put it into action is at hand. Thought without action will get us nowhere. Faith without action is the same. We even can make decisions, but until we act on them, they are worthless.

The Serenity Prayer is about action. The first line, "God, grant me the serenity," entails two specific actions. First, we must *connect*. Second, we must *ask*. When we can do this on a daily basis, because we get only a daily reprieve in life, only then will we know it is possible for us to change, to be coauthors of our lives.

Serenity Means Letting Go
of Drama in Our Lives

Serenity comes when we are willing to step off the stage, stop getting high on drama, and make the decision to live in reality and the truth of who we are.

There are those who believe that to live, to feel, to experience life is to live in stress, worry, frustration, and anger. When they are not feeling one or more of those things, they don't know what to feel, don't feel as if they are doing their job as a human being. Those negative emotions may make a person feel important, get them the attention they crave, but is that what life should be about?

Those same people will balk at the word *serenity,* tell themselves if they got that way, life would become boring, dull, and way too serious.

I was one of those people. When I was angry, with my actions I was saying, *Look at me, see my anger, know that someone has been unjust to me, and it's important.* When I was stressed, full of worry, the back of my hand would automatically be attached to my forehead, and if I'd been a Southern Belle, I'd have swooned. The truth was, when I did these things, I was saying, *See me, someone notice I exist, someone care about me,* because I wasn't able to care about myself and I didn't believe anyone else did. What a way to live.

Sometimes, I felt as if I'd been dropped off in a foreign land where I was the only one who didn't know the language. But with my dramatic expertise, I could convey those feelings of anger, frustration, stress, and worry without so much as saying a word. Yes, I was quite the drama queen. I didn't have a clue how to live and think like a "normal" person, and quite honestly, the idea of it put me off. I needed the drama to know I was alive, to know I could feel.

What does a person like that do with the idea of serenity, of becoming tranquil? Drama is like a drug. The more we use it, the more we need it, and the more extreme it becomes until it destroys our life. But the alternative, this serenity thing . . . I didn't know about that. It didn't sound like much fun.

What does a serene person do? For one thing, they can go to sleep at night without putting chemicals in their body. They don't worry about night terrors and nightmares. They don't wake up in the morning full of dread. They are not concerned with lies coming back on them, people confronting them about their actions.

Through a God of our understanding, just by asking for help, we are granted a way out. The door to serenity will open as if by magic, but we must be the one who walks through. God can do for us what we cannot do for ourselves, but we have to cooperate, do our part, or it won't happen.

The first step through that door can be a hard one to take. With that step, we are saying that what we thought, what we believed, what we've been doing wasn't working. We were wrong. That can be particularly difficult for someone like me, who never admitted I was wrong. It was terribly important to be right. Even when I knew I was wrong, I would argue until I was blue in the face that I was right.

Once we get over that first hurdle, it gets a bit easier. Obviously something wasn't working, or we wouldn't be seeking something else. The truth was, deep inside me, in that part that I never let anyone see, I wanted to be like other people, those folks who'd found some peace in their lives, but since I didn't believe that was possible, I simply told myself, and others, that I didn't need it; it would be boring, dull . . . no fun at all.

And I don't believe I could have found serenity by myself. It took some serious divine intervention to bring me to that point. I was told all I had to do was ask. Could anything be that simple? It was worth a try. How much worse could it get?

I stepped through the door. Boy, was I surprised at what I found on the other side. It was as if I'd lived in complete darkness my entire life and saw the sun for the first time. It shone on me, and the warmth soaked right through to my soul. And the sunlight ignited a fire within that has never been extinguished.

Serenity is exciting. It's much more exciting than living on the drama drug, a false existence in a made-up world. It's real life, and nothing is better than that. I no longer have to seek out attention, get noticed, do strange things to make others care for me. I care about myself, and the need for attention is gone. In my serenity there is absolutely nothing I need that I don't have.

With a God of my understanding in my corner, peace in my soul, and that fire for life in my heart, all things are possible. I get high on life, and the words *dull* and *boring* aren't a part of my vocabulary.

Be warned: Once you step through that door, it's hard to go back. I swear, a bulldozer couldn't move me back through that door. I love going to sleep at night, to be able to rest my body, mind, and soul. I can't wait to awaken in the morning, full of anticipation of what the new day will bring. It's a wonderful feeling to know that nothing, or no one, can steal my serenity. The only way to lose it is to give it up.

All we have to do is accept a God, ask for help, wait for the door to open, and step through. Serenity is waiting.

To Accept the Things
I Cannot Change

TO UNDERSTAND SERENITY through the acceptance of those things we can't change, we must first understand nonacceptance and the reasons for it. We see it, hear about it, read about it all the time. It shows itself in the form of frustration, anger, desperation, depression, even rage.

For many years, I could have been the poster child for nonacceptance and everything that went along with it. Sometimes, today, it's hard for me to reconcile the person I was with the person I am. It's almost like I've lived two entirely different lives. Those who didn't know me in my former life have a hard time imagining I was ever like that. Truth is, I was, and I make no secret of it.

Secrets do not foster serenity. In particular, self-secrets, the truth of who we are, hidden from the world, can be like a cancer that continues to grow until it overwhelms us. There is no freedom greater than having no secrets, nothing that can come back on us later, nothing hanging over our head that we believe could destroy us.

I grew up in a secret organization . . . called a family. Yes, we were the great guardians of the life we led. If no one knew, if we never said it out loud, it wasn't real. They called it privacy, but it was denial and non-acceptance of the truth.

I heard a story once about a family who lived in a small town. They were well-off financially, lived up to their social standings in the community. When their financial situation took a change for the worse, it was time to make some adjustments to their lifestyle. The husband and father of the family had great pride in his image, in how the world outside saw him. His pride was so great, in fact, that while the children and his wife went without, even to the point of going hungry, he put up his front for the world to see. The children would have been eligible for free lunches at school, but he wouldn't allow it. If he had, someone would have known their great secret. He simply refused to accept their change in circumstances.

I've thought about this man from time to time. I've wondered what he so feared that he could watch his family suffer. Did he fear losing the respect of those people he considered important? What about the respect and love of the family he was responsible for? What about his self-respect? I wondered, when he died, a lonely, bitter, old man, still clinging to the secrets with the last breath in his body, what was going through his mind?

Throughout our lives, circumstances change, situations come up over which we have no control. Our true character, who we truly are, shows through in how we accept the situation and how we deal with it. And it's not important what anyone else thinks about it. Only the feelings we are left with about ourselves matter.

By the time I was old enough to know better, I was a consummate liar. I would lie when it was easier to tell the truth. In fact, I told so many lies I began to believe them. The problem was the effort it took to remember who I'd told what. I usually had several lies lined up in my mind in case I got confused. I look back now and know that because I felt so powerless in my life, if I could lie and make someone believe me, at least for the moment, I was in control. The truth, and what I couldn't accept, was that I hated my life and I hated who I was.

My God, what would have happened if I admitted that? Would the world have come to an end? No, but mine would have. If I'd said it out loud, accepted the truth, I might have felt compelled to actually *do* something about it. I wouldn't be ready for that scenario for many years.

There are many schools of thought on whether our path in life is determined by fate, by choice, or guided by the hand of God or perhaps just by the luck of the draw. For years, I believed the last, and obviously, I hadn't won the jackpot. Oh, I'd smile and say the right things, but inside lived a mean-spirited, ugly human being who resented everything. It didn't matter whether someone had better clothes, a home, a nicer family, more money, a better job, a cuter boyfriend, was prettier, slimmer, had nicer hair—someone else always had something that was better, bigger, or more desirous than I had. It wasn't my fault. I wasn't pretty because of my parents. I wasn't rich because of my circumstances. I wasn't nice because no one was nice to me. My call to arms became, "Why *me?* Why not *me?* What about *me?*"

My justification for thinking the world should revolve around me was that my needs were not met as a child. Nobody loved me. They were mean to me. I never got the things I wanted. My life was a mess. What did they expect?

I may not have had a choice of the life I was born into, but there came a day when I did. I chose to hang onto the past, the resentments, the rage, until it nearly killed me. At the least, it made my life a daily exercise in misery. And the misery resulted in all manner of self-destructive behavior.

The past is a big deal. We cannot change it. It's done; it's over; we can't go back and do it over. However, if the past is still influencing our life, our choices, how do we find acceptance? Acceptance will come through a new understanding, a different perception of where we have been, what has happened to us and others.

It's obvious when we are still influenced by the past, still holding on to old resentments, regrets, anger. It shows itself in addictions: the alcoholic or drug addict who seeks oblivion from their thoughts and memories; the gambler who escapes into a world of bells and whistles, the sound of coins hitting metal when they win; the overeater who comforts themselves with taste and texture of foods, ever seeking to feel better as they destroy their self-esteem; the smoker who puffs away, trying to calm themselves, to cope with life. There are even healthy obsessions that are nonetheless obsessions, avenues of escape: people become workaholics, obsessive cleaners, feel compelled to help others to avoid looking at their own lives. But no matter how one goes about avoidance, it is only a temporary solution to a persistent problem.

The first step toward recovery from the past is to accept it for what it was. A dear friend gave me a tip to help me find a way. She said, "Name it, claim it, and let it go."

Name It

Words are a powerful force in our lives. They are how we express what we think, feel, and believe. Imagine what it would be like to go through just one day without speaking—and no, you can't write it down. The words would well up inside us like a big balloon with nowhere to go.

When we are not honest with ourselves or with others, that's pretty much what happens. It's like when we say the right things, or the things we think others want to hear, while all the time our mind is telling us something entirely different. Did you ever wonder what would happen if you said what you really thought?

Often times, when we are lacking serenity, it's caused by the words we are using, or not using, to understand ourselves and others. Once when I went to a friend to talk over a specific problem I was having, she asked, "What do you think is going on?" My reply was that I was confused. To my surprise, she said, "Well, isn't that handy."

After I got over being appalled at her response, when I had time to think about it, she made sense. Saying I was "confused" gave me an excuse not to confront the problem, not to deal with it. I knew what I thought, I knew what I wanted to do, but I lacked the courage to do it. It was much easier to place the back of my hand on my forehead, cry "confused," and do nothing.

To find resolution to any problem, the first step is to recognize the problem. To do that, we need to give it a name. Then, we need to put a name to how we are feeling. When I was a few years into recovery from addiction, and still attempting to resolve those things from the past that kept me unhappy, I struggled with this idea of naming the problem. Most of my struggle occurred because I didn't like the words I would have to use that applied to me.

I thought I'd dealt with a lot of my past issues, but I found myself unable to resolve the deaths of my children. I just couldn't let it go. I'd like to tell you it was because I was so full of love, so filled with grieving that I couldn't get past it, but that would be a lie. I was full of anger—

unexpressed anger. It went back to my cry in the night. "Why *me?*"

The truth was, it wasn't about the children. It was about me. The realization was that I'd used the deaths of my children to become a martyr. I held onto that initial pain as an excuse to do any destructive thing I wanted and to feel justified. I needed a reason to be a failure, to remain unhappy, not to allow anyone to have expectations of me. You see, it's easier to be a failure, but I always had to have an excuse outside of myself.

Claim It

It was easier for me to blame others and life situations that were out of my control than to admit I had any part in the problem.

I recall some of the rationalizations I handed myself. I didn't have a good childhood foundation to pull from. I was genetically predisposed to addiction. Nobody liked me. I wasn't pretty. I wasn't smart. I wasn't going to amount to anything, so why try. If there was a God, he probably hated me—I mean, look at the life he'd given me. I was sure most of it was his fault. "Why *me?*"

What I learned was, *Why not me?* What made me think I should be the one who escapes the problems in life? Did I think I was better than those other people who lived through their tragedies?

I learned that people don't wake up one day and decide who to be. They are the result of their life experiences. The people involved in raising me probably did the best they could with what they had to work with. I got raised. I was fed, clothed, and sheltered until I was old enough to do it for myself. I had the choice to learn from what I saw or fall into the same traps as them. I chose the latter. Even as a child, I knew the problems alcohol and drugs caused, but I was the one who put the bottle to my lips, who chose to take that first drink, to swallow that first pill. No one held it to my mouth.

What I had to claim was responsibility for my own choices and choosing to live with self-pity, excuses, and blaming others. If I couldn't find anyone else to blame, it had to be God's fault.

Poor God. I must have given him fits. I cursed him, hated him, blamed him, and denied him access to my life. He must have looked at me and just shook his head and told himself it was time to take me down to the bare essentials and simply start over. And that's pretty much what happened.

I was offered a second chance in life, and I took it. But if I were to succeed, to find that serenity that had escaped me for so many years, I would have to accept my past as a part of who I am and understand the choices that I made were made—I couldn't go back and change them. However,

I didn't have to repeat them. I was given a new day to find a new way.

It wasn't that I wasn't pretty, smart, or capable, but that I chose to believe it was so. It wasn't that I couldn't do things, but the fear of failure and rejection kept me from trying. I can remember saying I wasn't afraid of anything, but that was just the face I put on for others. Anyone who puts the kinds of things in their body that I did in mine is full of fear, or they wouldn't have to do it.

It was time to claim what belonged to me: selfishness, self-pity, irresponsibility, blaming others for my mistakes, escape into addictions, and fear. They were the words that told me who I was and why I had no peace in my life. Once said aloud, accepted as my truth, I'd found a starting point.

We cannot change the past, but we have today, this moment, and the choice to do it differently. We can see the past as a great learning experience that will teach us better how to live today. To deny the past is to deny ourselves. We are the sum total of all our life up to this exact moment in time.

Let It Go

Letting it go isn't about denying the past. It isn't about trying to bury it so deep that we think it can't come back to haunt us. It's about the freedom we will know once it's faced head-on and resolved.

Once we've recognized a situation in truth, put a name to it, and accepted our part in it—claimed it—letting go may require action. It's one thing to be sorry for something hurtful we have done and another thing entirely to resolve it.

Since I had been like a tornado, ripping through the lives of others, not caring about the destruction I left in my wake, this would be a big proposition. The first thing that came to my mind was, *What about me? What about what they did to me?* Old habits die hard.

What I discovered was, it didn't matter what anyone else did. What was important was how I acted. After all, they don't have to live inside me, don't have to live with my regrets, don't have to toss and turn at night, the nightmares so bad that I was afraid to go to sleep. They aren't the ones who had to face me in the mirror each morning and deal with the disgust I felt.

And so, it began. One by one, I considered those things that still lived in my mind from the past and what I could do about them. Through this experience, I came to know that the closer the relationship with another person is, the harder it is to take the action required.

One of my most difficult situations was with my father. As a child, I loved him, adored him. He was my hero. I remember when he worked for the railroad. I would stay awake listening for him to come in. Then, I'd sneak out of bed and share sardines and crackers with him in the kitchen. But that changed. My parents divorced. Still quite young, I didn't understand divorce. The only thing I knew was he left *me*. He abandoned *me*. My cry in the night began very young.

Over the years, when I thought that others took my place in his life, I began to punish him any way I could. I said hurtful things. I did anything I could to upset his life. I blamed him for everything. Even though my mother remarried and years had passed when she shot herself, I blamed him.

I convinced myself he didn't love me. Gee, I wonder why, when I was so lovable. Anyway, the time came when I think he just gave up on me, gave up the hope there would ever be any kind of decent relationship for us. I hadn't had contact with him in some time.

No matter how much I denied it, the things I'd done, the hateful words spoken in anger, the lack of a relationship, bothered me . . . lived in me every day and were still affecting my life. What to do? It was the most difficult letter I've ever written. For the first time, I told my father the truth. I admitted my deepest feelings, my shame, my guilt, how sorry I was for my part in things. I apologized. I finally understood that when he left, it wasn't about me. It was about him and my mother . . . that everything in life was not about me.

He didn't respond for a time. I can't tell you how nervous I was when the first letter appeared, and the weight lifted from my shoulders, from my very soul, when he was kind, compassionate, and caring. We wrote to each other for a time, then talked on the phone, and finally began to see each other again. The point is, without action, without putting myself out there, telling the truth with no expectations, it would never have been resolved. I would have never been able to let it go.

Even if my father had made the choice not to forgive, not to pursue a relationship with me, it would have still been resolved. When I wrote the letter, I'd accepted that scenario as a possibility. All I could do was live in the truth, share it with him, and accept whatever his decision was. I'm grateful it turned out the way it did, but again, either way, I would have been able to let it go.

There were many more to come. I wrote letters; I visited people and situations from my past; I talked to tombstones; I prayed to a God of my understanding; I paid back money I owed; and I even had to return something I'd taken from another. Some people were kind, others not so much. But it didn't matter how they reacted. It only mattered that I'd become willing to take the required action, with the truth in my heart and my words. It wasn't about them, what they'd done or said, and I didn't attempt to justify what I'd done. I'd just admit it and ask for forgiveness. Whether or not they gave it was their choice, and I certainly couldn't blame them if they didn't.

What a relief! However, there was another hurdle to clear. There was still one person whom I had to deal with. I had to find a way to forgive myself. Once I'd put a name to those things I'd done, the true feelings I had, claimed my part in them, they were a part of me. They were real. I'd done some pretty horrible things. I'm sure I broke all of the commandments, except murder, and that just didn't come up. Believe me, I'd done it in thought, if not in deed. The truth of my life was nearly overwhelming. How would I ever forgive myself?

Through a strange set of circumstances, I ended up at a spiritual retreat run by two priests who were in recovery from addiction. In one of their talks, I heard the answer. They said, "When you have truly gone to a God of your understanding, and asked for forgiveness, and refuse to forgive yourself, you have set yourself above God." Had I really done that? Had I set myself above God? It began to make sense.

The following day, when I had the opportunity to speak with one of the priests, one on one, he said something that will be etched in my mind forever. He said, "Any time you hang onto something that hard, that causes you that much pain, you are getting something out of it. You must decide what that is." It was like someone hit me in the head with a brick. The reason I hadn't let go of the pain, the past, was that *if I ever burned my bridges, I'd never have an excuse left to go back*. From that point on, I had no reason not to become the best person I could be, to be a success in life. I let it go.

To find serenity through acceptance is to revisit your life, what lives in you from the past — not the actions of others, but your thoughts, words, and deeds. What keeps you up at night, enters your dreamtime? Why do you keep feeding the pain? What are you getting out of it? Are you willing to do what it takes to find resolution? Not easy questions to answer, but the truth will most certainly set you free.

Today, through this process, I can rest when I sleep. I can look at myself in the mirror, and even though I'm aging, no longer young and pretty, I think I'm beautiful. I can see past the wrinkles and age spots to the person I really am. Every day I'm granted, I give myself to a God of my under-standing and try to be the best person I can be. I'm not perfect by any means, but thank God, I don't have to be. At least today I know when I make a mistake, do something hurtful, create a bad situation, there's a way to deal with it. I name it, claim it, and let it go.

We don't have to go in search of all those things we did in our life to clean out the rubbish of the past. In becom-ing honest with ourselves, we will know those things that truly bother us.

For instance, years ago, as I left a motel in the wee hours of the morning, I took a potted plant. I know that happened. I know I was a thief. However, it wasn't something that kept me up at night. It wasn't what made me hate myself. It was simply one of those things I'd done that I couldn't go back and change. It would have to be enough to admit it to myself, feel bad about it, ask God to forgive me, and let it go.

I'm sure there have been a great many people I've offended in the course of my life, from waitresses to cab drivers. I was an offensive person. I can't look them all up, didn't know most of their names, but I can do better today. I can be kind, considerate, and caring of the feelings of others in my daily dealings with them.

While I'm cleansing my soul, I must always consider the feelings of others. Realistically, what good would it do anyone if I go admit to another woman that I slept with her husband? To bring her pain, simply to purge my soul, would be just as wrong as what I did in the first place. Again, the point is, once I understand what I did, that it was wrong for me, not to do it ever again.

We will not have to hunt for those things from the past that are keeping us from serenity. When we are ready for a new way to live, to seek happiness and peace, they will show themselves in the truth of who we are. When we are ready to walk through, the doors will open, the teachers will appear.

Accepting Other People

How many mental patients does it take to change a light bulb? One, but he has to really want to change it.

I heard that joke from another patient during my incarceration in a mental hospital. I was twenty-six years old when I came to, strapped hand and foot to a bed, deemed a danger to myself and others. When I tried desperately to explain to them that I wasn't crazy, I just had too much to drink and was acting crazy, they didn't listen. When I refused to cooperate, they hooked me up to electricity. I can tell you, I made some really poor choices during that period in my life, and I paid dearly for them.

They gave me drugs. They gave me shock therapy. They spoke to me of my behavior. Finally, they let me out, under certain conditions. I had to take medication and go to therapy on a regular basis. Having made the decision that I would rather die than live like a slobbering fool, unable to think, I flushed the pills, but I did go to therapy.

Things moved along very quickly. Since I hadn't finished high school, I attained my GED and started college. Fascinated with the human condition, especially my own, I chose psychology. Yes, I'd lived through it all, knew all the answers, and would be the person to lead you all out of bondage . . . mental bondage anyway. What a laugh! The only thing I learned of any true value through my college experience was that I wasn't stupid. I was teachable.

I couldn't stay in school and therapy forever. Eventually, I would be required to get back out there, deal with life and other people. Other people—the bane of my existence. "They" were the reason for all my problems. They hadn't done what I wanted, the way I wanted it, when I wanted it. There were certain ways that parents, friends, lovers, children should act, and they'd failed. I was the result of their failure to live up to my expectations.

They made me crazy. If it hadn't been for them, I wouldn't have had to drink, to take drugs. While in my mode of trying to change everyone into what I thought they should be, one very important fact eluded me. In all my relationships there was one common denominator. It was me. Many of the people in my life didn't know each other, but they were all acquainted with me.

From the time of my release from the hospital, it would take nearly ten years before I realized that I was the problem. I'd been analyzed, theorized, drugged, hooked up to electricity, educated in the study of human behavior, but one sentence from a friend made the difference. I'd run through everyone in my life, except this one woman, my only friend. She said, "You have a problem." She told me the truth and walked away.

When I eventually accepted the truth about myself, it was the beginning of a life lesson that would teach me about the acceptance of other people.

Other people can be our greatest joy or our biggest frustration in life, depending solely on our outlook. We want to be loved and accepted for who we are, but are we willing to give that same privilege to others?

I was constantly trying to make others understand, to explain myself, to justify my actions, to get others to validate my life and choices. What I didn't understand was that they couldn't. It was like trying to tell someone who had never experienced it what it felt like to give birth. No one had lived my life, gone through my personal experiences, but me. I was putting unrealistic expectations on people. They couldn't understand me any more than I could understand them. However, the truth was that it wasn't necessary to understand . . . simply to accept.

When we come to believe there is a power greater than ourselves in the universe, that there is a plan, reasons of which we may be unaware, and we are a part of it, then we must acknowledge that others are as well. If we believe we are exactly where we are supposed to be, doing what we are supposed to do, then we must grant the same to other people. If that is true, what makes us think God needs our help in the process?

For example, the woman who told me I had a problem didn't try to change me, tell me what I should do, or lead me out of my misery. She simply stated what she believed to be true, and by walking away, said what I was doing was unacceptable to her. To maintain her own serenity, she made the choice to eliminate me from her life.

And that's what we are talking about here: maintaining our serenity through acceptance of others' rights to make their own life choices. We can't change other people. Even if we can convince them to change their behavior to suit us, what have we accomplished? Because that person is living against themselves, their true nature, is not being true to themselves, there will be a very unhappy, frustrated, angry person inside. Eventually that person will show who they really are, along with the resentments about the expectations imposed on them.

After college, I got married again. My oldest son and I moved to Florida with my new husband. He was quite the mover and shaker, and certainly was into impressing others. Obviously he'd impressed me. I married him after swearing I'd never get married again. But there I was.

He decided to make me over in his image. He wanted his daughters to take me shopping, get my hair done better, teach me what it meant to be his wife and what was expected of me. I went along with it for a while.

He loved to entertain. There would be a dinner party one evening at our house on the beach. Before he left for the day, he gave me very explicit instructions. I was to go to the fish market and pick up an order of blue crab. The man at the market would explain how to prepare them. I could do that, I thought. But it wasn't as easy as it sounded.

Back at the house, I followed the man's instructions. He said put the crabs on ice while I got the boiling water ready. I threw a few ice cubes in the sink and dumped the bucket of creatures on top. Suddenly, there was a great deal of activity. They were everywhere, crawling out of the sink, onto the cabinet, scooting across the floor. Afraid to touch them, I tried using two wooden spoons to capture them. When I finally got most of them in the sink, and the water boiling, I picked one up between my spoons. I tried to stop, but he slipped into the water. I heard a scream.

I'd had no idea about the noise it made when air escaped from the shell. As I watched the crab turn red, the realization that I'd killed him sunk in. My God, what had I done? I didn't believe in hurting any living thing. I turned the water off, removed the poor dead crab, gathered the rest of them into the bucket, and headed for the beach. After a very small funeral for the dead crab, as I buried him under the sand, I took the clamps off the claws, and one by one, released the others back to the ocean. As I watched them scurry to freedom, I wept for what I'd done, for the one who wouldn't return to a life of freedom, at least from me.

I returned to the house. I put on my bib overalls, my favorite thing to wear, dug out my jelly glass, the one I drank out of when no one was around, and that's how my husband found me—dressed inappropriately, drinking from the forbidden jar, and no crabs for dinner. Like the crabs, I freed myself from a life of bondage, scurried back to Illinois and a life I could live with.

My husband didn't love me. He loved an idea. He knew I couldn't kill things. I had trouble swatting flies. He knew I didn't care about impressing other people. But he also knew I was trying to find a better life for my son and myself. In my desperation to not fail at another marriage, to please another person, I allowed him to change me. However, the crabs told the story. That he would expect me to go against the very core of who I was was too much. I left that day.

Today, I understand that when we care for someone, or they care for us, to know serenity in the relationship, we must accept each person's right to be who they are. When we find that we are constantly explaining ourselves, making excuses for the person we are, attempting to justify our actions, and walking on eggshells to avoid the wrath of another, or expecting another person to do that, there is a problem.

Acceptance means exactly that: accepting the other person in their totality. It's about saying, "I don't have to agree with everything you do, but I would fight for your right to do it, to think it, to believe it, to live your life in your own truth."

If we cannot accept other people and their rights, we need to stay away from them, not try to change them. We will not be liked and accepted by everyone; neither will we like or accept everyone. It's unrealistic to believe that will happen. It's all right if you don't like me, don't like the way I live my life. You have a choice not to be a part of it.

I had a friend once who told me how he knew he had arrived at serenity. He said that if someone walked up to him on the street and said, "I think you're a dirty bastard and I can't stand you," his answer would be to smile and say, "Well, thank you for your opinion. Have a nice day." He'd truly accepted his right to live his life, unencumbered by the expectations of others, and had learned that no matter what he did, there would be others who didn't like him. And that was their choice. It didn't have to affect his life or cause him to make any changes he didn't find necessary.

You cannot change another person any more than they can change you. We may change behavior patterns from time to time to please others, but who we really are lives on. I may dress up, drink out of fine stemware, but there still lives in me that very common person who prefers bib overalls and a jelly glass, that person who, like the crabs, wants nothing more than to live out my life as me ... totally free.

Imagine what it would be like to be debt free. The feeling is even more profound when we are free of emotional debt, when we arrive at the point of believing we don't "owe" anyone, anything, any more—nor do they owe us. Our only concerns need to be a God of our choosing, the laws of the land, and ourselves.

From that moment on, anything we give to another must be with an open hand and an open heart, simply because it is what we want to do. There will be no expectations of paybacks, no building up points to make another person feel they owe us.

This attitude will carry over into the smallest things in our lives. Household chores are a good example. Just because a person is a wife doesn't mean she must do certain chores, or do them on a schedule imposed by another. If she doesn't want to make the beds or do the dishes, the person who is bothered by unmade beds and a sink full of dishes should do it. Point is, she should have a choice. Now, if the other person involved can't live with her choices, perhaps he hasn't made the best choice for a wife. And the same applies to men. If he prefers to watch a football game rather than work in the yard, the wife has a choice. If it bothers her, she can do it, or she can hire someone to do it. It's all a matter of choices. When we accept the right to make our own, we must give that same right to others.

Who lives like that? You might be surprised. I live that way, and I know there are many other people who do. Even today, after eighteen years of marriage, when I fix supper, my husband still says, "Thank you." I don't try to convince him to do anything he doesn't want to do. Why would I do that? I certainly don't want him doing it to me.

We are grown-up people who don't feel the need to make up excuses for how we feel, what we do; we have stopped attempting to explain ourselves to everyone, and we understand the only justification necessary is to ourselves. It's enough to say, "Yes" or "No" to a situation, another person, knowing it's our right.

Think of the things you are doing that you don't want to do, the things you might be insisting another person do to please you. Now, think about how you feel afterward. My guess is, they feel the same way. That's not serenity. True love, caring for another person, is about acceptance of ourselves and others. It is knowing that we all want to be accepted as we are. To change or not to change is an individual right. To understand acceptance of the things we cannot change, to find serenity through that understanding, is to know we have the choice to accept or not accept. We have the choice to feel free to choose, to feel serenity, as do others. There is no greater feeling than when we free ourselves from emotional bondage. Game over. We win.

Acceptance Means Letting Go of Expectations

Serenity comes from accepting ourselves, our choice to live the life we were given; accepting the past for what it was, knowing that we can't change it but that we can learn from it; and not putting expectations on others.

There are two kinds of people in the world. There are those who have learned to accept the inevitable in life, and those who live in a constant struggle, believing they can figure out a way to change things. The former know peace, the latter know only frustration and anger.

Realistically speaking, certain things are facts that apply to all people. We are born to whatever family we get and to the circumstances of that group of people. Stuff happens to everyone, no matter their situation. None of us can escape life. Even if we were dropped off on a desert island as a child, never had to deal with other people, certain things would still happen. While we are growing up, we will not handle everything well. There will be mistakes, regrets, resentments, and along with all the wonderful things in our life, they will form our past.

Our past can enhance our lives by teaching us valuable life lessons, or it can hinder our lives because it lives in our minds today, affecting the way we conduct ourselves. Either way, the past can't be changed. The only thing we can change about the past is our perception of it. It's like that old story about parents. When we were teenagers, we saw them as stupid, not with it. When we got older, we were amazed how much they'd learned. Those who are prone to personal growth understand that what was true for us at age fifteen is no longer true at eighteen, twenty-five, thirty, fifty, eighty. Our truths change as we change, and aging is inevitable.

The aging process continues no matter what we do. Plastic surgery can keep the body appearing younger than it is; diet and exercise may keep us fit; scientists are continually figuring out how to keep us going longer; but we are still the age we are, and in the end, we will all die. We never know the time of our death unless we bring it on ourselves. The terminally ill may have a better idea when they are going, but even that is not for certain.

So, here we are, stuck in this life for a certain amount of time, with no way of knowing if it will be today, tomorrow, or fifty years from now, but we are all going. A great deal of our time here will be spent interacting with other people. There will be parents, children, teachers, bosses, love interests, spouses, friends, and foes. That's a lot of interaction, and considering the differences in people, it will require a lot of skill.

Because other people are so important in our lives, our expectations of how they should be can cause our greatest struggles. People have a tendency to do what they want, the way they want, when they want, and we can end up disillusioned, disappointed, and frustrated, even filled with anger. We may blame others for our feelings, but the truth is, we are responsible for our own feelings, how we react to others' actions.

It's hard not to have expectations of others, especially when they are a part of our lives. Again, it is a matter of perception. How can we expect anyone to be who they are not, to ask them to act in ways that goes against the very core of their being? Each person, including ourselves, is the sum total of their life, their experiences, circumstances, life lessons, and they should have the right to follow their own path in life. Their path might intersect ours, but we must all travel in our own way.

When we believe we can change the way others think, feel, and what they do, we are asking for frustration. When we think we can grab hold of them and drag them down our path with us, our way, we will find ourselves coupled with an unhappy, uncooperative individual who will do everything in their power to make our life miserable.

When we feel powerful only as a result of exerting power over others, there's a problem, and the problem is within us. The truly powerful have learned either to accept people the way they are and allow them to be a part of their lives, or to stay away from them but still accept their right to be. They have learned to stay in their own business and leave others, and God, to theirs.

It's not necessary for me to understand other people's relationships, what occupations they choose, the way they choose to live. It might not be for me, but God knows I don't have to live their life, die with their memories, regrets, or happinesses. If I want them to be a part of my life, to have a good relationship, we need to accept each other the way we are. If we can't, or refuse to do that, it's time to move on.

One example of living without expectations is about holidays. When my husband and I got married, he told me he didn't like the idea of being forced into buying gifts just because it was a certain day of the year. He might come home on a Tuesday, in the middle of May, with a wonderful surprise for me, but it was because he wanted to do it, not because he was expected to. And it makes the gift twice as wonderful. That may seem like a little thing, but if I'd insisted that we follow tradition, I'm sure he would have resented every gift he felt forced to find and purchase. Do I feel bad when other wives tell me what their husbands got them for Christmas, their anniversary or birthday? Not at all. When they ask what I received, I just smile that secret smile and tell them nothing at all.

When we are able to live in acceptance of those things we can't change, we will know a new freedom, and we will find others are drawn to us in a different way. Because they don't feel judged, because we never expect any more of them than they want to give, to be, there will be a level of comfort and open sharing we've never before experienced.

I'm trying to become as smart as my dogs, who accept me at my best and my worst, who don't care how I look, how I live my life. They expect nothing of me more than I want to give and are happy to be a part of my life. Ah, that we could all be that accepting.

Courage to Change
the Things I Can

COURAGE ISN'T ABOUT being fearless. It's about overcoming fear, moving past it to the other side. When a person runs into a burning house to save someone, it's not that he doesn't fear getting burned or dying, but he believes the result is worth the effort. It's worth the risk.

That's called "catastrophic courage." That's not the kind of courage the Serenity Prayer is talking about. The prayer speaks to us of the courage it takes, on a daily basis, to live our life in an unsure world.

There are so many things to fear. As many humans as live on this planet, there are probably as many fears. However, some fears are more common to a greater group of people. Consider these:

- The fear of rejection/judgment
- The fear of loneliness/being alone
- The fear of love/commitment
- The fear of failure/success
- The fear of the unknown

Any of the fears listed can keep our lives paralyzed. Thoreau said, "Most men lead lives of quiet desperation." I've always believed it is fear that keeps them quiet. The question is, Do we have the power, the courage, to change these fears, those things that keep us from serenity?

Fear of Rejection/Judgment

We live in a world of illusion, delusion, a world where image can take on great importance . . . if we allow it. Being overly concerned with the image we project to the world can cause us to do things, say things, create situations that are false. Then we have the never-ending job of maintenance.

No matter what image we have chosen to project, regardless of our ability to maintain it, and even though we may be getting great accolade from others, if it is false, our life will be based in fear of rejection and judgment by others.

When I think of image, I think of my mother. She was a beautiful, petite woman who loved to be around other people. She loved to party, to laugh, to smile, to make others see her as the light that brightened any room. You can only imagine how stunned her friends, her coworkers, even her family members were when she put a gun to her body and pulled the trigger. At age thirty-nine, she was dead.

I can only speculate about my mother. Even though she raised me, I'm not sure I ever really knew her. I knew facts about her life, but not the person, so carefully guarded she was. There were glimpses from time to time, those unguarded moments when I saw a different side of her ... the sadness, unhappiness.

The morning of the day she died, I arrived at her house to find her crying at the kitchen table. When I asked her what was wrong, she brushed away the tears and said, "I'm tired, that's all.... Just so tired." I thought she meant tired from working, from trying to keep the house up ... that sort of thing.

I think what she was trying to tell me was that she was tired of life, tired of keeping up appearances, exhausted with living in a constant state of compromise. I choose to believe that when she pulled the trigger, she hoped to go to a better place ... a place where she could be free of the constraints she thought the world, and others, imposed on her. I hope that's what she found.

It's odd—I always saw her as courageous, daring, able to throw herself into situations others would fear. I came to understand, her courage came in one bottle or another— pills, alcohol, or the combination. And for many years I believed that's where courage came from. But it wasn't about finding courage, it was about numbing fear.

I chose her way to numb the fear, but that was all it was ... numb. It always returned because it lived within me, was as much a part of me as the skin I wore. I nearly numbed myself to death worrying about fitting in with this group, or that, or some person whom I wanted to like me, to attain that sense of belonging, to find my place in the great scheme of things. But I was walking alone.

It wasn't until I connected to a God of my understanding that I understood. I didn't have to be someone I wasn't to fit in. I belonged because God said so when he made me, allowed me a life here. How I looked in the eyes of others didn't matter. I was his beautiful creation, and he could see into my heart. There was no hiding or image that he couldn't see through. I never had to walk alone as long as I kept that connection on a daily basis.

Others must come to their own life choices, just as I did. Whether they reject me or embrace me is not contingent on what I do, how I look, if I can wow them with brilliant conversation, or project an image with which they wish to be associated. Their judgments need not affect my life, the person I am, or the actions I take. The courage to face the fear of rejection and judgment of others is deciding what you see is what you get. I am that I am. I like myself, and nothing you can say or do can change that.

It's a risk, there's no doubt about it, to put ourselves out there just as we are. But like the man who runs into the burning building, the results are worth it. The life we save will be our own. Maybe all courage really is catastrophic. It's all relative. If our life is a catastrophe, for whatever reason, the same amount of courage will be required.

There are times it is more difficult to save ourselves than to save others. It's like being a conscientious objector during times of war. Some will take that stand with the knowledge there will be those who judge them harshly, call them names, even condemn them for their beliefs. There will be others who will run away to hide who they are, in fear of the consequences. Then, there are the ones who find a way to stuff away the truth of who they are, what they believe and do what is expected of them. They may avoid the harsh judgment of others, not have to face rejections, but can never escape the judgment they put on themselves. It takes great courage of our convictions to make a stand on an unpopular idea.

It's much safer to stand behind the convictions, the beliefs of another. That way, we always have an out. It's like saying *he* wanted to do it. It wasn't *my* idea. It releases us from blame, from censure by others.

The way to overcome the fear of rejection and judgment by others is to be true to what you really believe is right for you. If you must change your behavior, the way you think and act, even the way you look, to please another, you are living against yourself. No one who lives that way can find peace and serenity, let alone happiness.

The result of taking a stand is a feeling of freedom like no other. Try it for one day. Say what you mean, what you think, all day. Don't hold back, or the experiment won't work. Don't go out looking for things and people whom you have disagreed with in the past but hadn't taken a stand with. Simply pick a day, and for that one day be as honest as you can with yourself and others. See how you feel at the end of that day. I would be amazed if you didn't like yourself better.

It's about taking back your self-respect. After all, if you had a friend who lived their life in lies and falsehoods, would you respect them? If your spouse spent all their time and energy in an effort to impress others, doing things they didn't want for people they didn't even care about, how would you see them? Look in the mirror and ask the same questions about yourself. Do you like what you see? If not, do you have the courage to face the fear that keeps you from changing?

I always think, "What's the worst thing that can happen if I say what I really think, do what I really want to do?" And in the deepest part of me, I know what those things are. When I waffle, it's because I don't want to deal with possible consequences. Questions pop into my mind. What will people think? What if I hurt another's feelings? What if they don't like me anymore? Those questions are nothing more than excuses not to make the hard choices, do the right thing for myself. And I get to blame them. Isn't that handy!

When we live from the soul, the truth, we stop making assumptions about how others will react and simply give them the right to their feelings, to their reactions, and accept it. That's not something we can change. The changes have to take place within us. When they do, they will show in our actions, in our state of mind. We will understand what real courage, lived out every day, means. It means we can overcome whatever it takes and continue to believe there is goodness and great meaning to life.

Fear of Loneliness/Being Alone

Have you ever had that feeling that life is you against the world? Do you think no one knows, no one understands? Have you stood in the middle of a social gathering and knew you didn't belong there, were the one who didn't fit in? That's loneliness. Did you stay because you couldn't stand the thought of going home to no one? That's fear of being alone.

Loneliness is a feeling, but being alone is a reality. It is the absence of others. We can combat being alone simply by putting ourselves out there, around other people. But the feeling of loneliness lives within and travels with us wherever we go, no matter how many people we're around.

I was very seldom alone, but I was always lonely. No matter how far I ran, how fast, with whom, every time I stopped to take a breath, there it was . . . the same empty feeling. It was like everyone else was given the handbook about life, except me. That's why I hated being alone. In those moments, with no distractions, the truth would be revealed in bits and pieces.

I'd gone from being someone's daughter, to a teenaged mother, to a girlfriend and wife many times over. I was a student, then an employee. However, I wasn't a person in my own right. I was born to the club, but they forgot to give me the book, to explain to me how to accomplish a real life, be a part of the lives of others. So, I withdrew my membership.

I started my own club. I was the only member, and the membership fee was great loneliness. I said that I didn't need you . . . any of you. I could make it on my own. The truth was, I didn't think you wanted me, so it was easier to say, "I don't need you." That became my club motto.

Today, I know that in my quest to survive, to avoid pain, to never be alone, it only made my loneliness more apparent. I wanted to be with you, but not be a part of you. Initiation to the humanity club would be to face my fear of being alone, the overwhelming feeling of loneliness. It would be a road to self-discovery. I wasn't sure I was ready to travel that road.

The first step on the journey to self-discovery is the realization of our fear. One of my greatest fears was that if I joined you, cared about you, the day would come that I would lose you. Then, the pain would come. In my desperation to avoid the pain, I brought on my other fears: loneliness and fear of being alone.

It's absolutely amazing the lengths we will go to not to be alone. We will spend time with people we don't like, in places we don't want to be, doing things we don't want to do. It seems any person, any activity is better than being alone with our thoughts, memories, or whatever it is we are trying to avoid. Wouldn't it be wonderful if there were a book with all the answers? Actually, there are many books full of answers, written by people who are wise in the ways of life, full of sage advice. I read books. They stimulated me intellectually. I sought out those in the know. I listened and understood where they were in life, but I still didn't understand how they got there. The fear lived on.

One consistent message that I received over and over was that I would never be happy with other people, would never overcome the loneliness, until I was happy by myself. To change would require facing my fear head-on, taking risks I hadn't been willing to take in years. I would have to get involved, not only in the lives of others, but in my own life.

Getting involved required trust. My past experiences taught me not to trust. Others had deserted me, hurt me, died on me. At times the pain was so big, it was nearly tangible. Because of my reaction to the pain, I no longer trusted my instincts. After all, they got me where I was . . . alone and lonely. Holding onto the past, shielding myself with fear kept me safe from pain caused by others, but it was nothing compared to the pain I caused myself.

The choice was mine. Could I put myself out there, allow the world to see who I really was? When we think no one knows how we feel, no one understands us, it's usually because we don't allow it. They can't know if we don't let them in, don't tell them. When you hear people talk about being "born again," I think this must be what they mean. I reentered the world at age thirty-five as the real me.

That's called "walking through the fear." Remember, courage is not about being fearless, but about overcoming fear. It was scary. What if you didn't like me? What if I tried to join your club and found I wasn't welcome?

What I discovered was that some people liked me, some didn't. I wasn't all that different from the rest of you. We all had our skeletons, our fears, individual pasts to deal with. I'd begun to look at the similarities instead of the differences. It seemed that I'd spent a lifetime comparing my insides with everyone else's outsides, so I always came up short. When I got to know you, allowed myself to listen, I began to understand.

The life lesson I learned through these new experiences with other people was that unless I open up to others, show them the truth of who I am, I can't expect it from them.

When I stopped playing the "I'm fine" game, where I paste a smile on my face and pretend everything is fine, fine, fine, others didn't feel the need to play . . . to pretend.

The beginning of change was to be myself, warts and all, to put it out there, and to allow others to make the choice whether they wanted to be a part of my life or to allow me into theirs—or not. I was involved. I was making choices. I was attempting to trust my instincts. And my instincts told me I wanted to belong, to be a part of the human race. I wanted to love and be loved. I wanted to live in reality, to know what it felt like to be comfortable with others.

What I found is that it is easier to become involved in the lives of others than it is in one's own life. It's absolutely amazing how clearly we can see others' problems and the solutions to them, but not see our own. Why is that? Perhaps it's because we are not the ones who have to walk through their fears to make the changes.

A friend once suggested to me that when I had a problem, I should imagine another person coming to me with the same problem. What would I advise that person to do? That's exactly what *I* need to do. When we look at it from another perspective, we might be more careful of the advice we throw out there. Think what it would be like to follow our own advice.

It may sound selfish, but I believe that to overcome loneliness, we have to focus on ourselves, on the changes we need to make. Only then will we truly be of use to others. If we are not happy, content human beings, what makes us think we can tell anyone else how to be?

At last, I had friends, was accepted by others as I was, found some self-respect. The loneliness was held at bay by filling my time with friends, new activities. It worked, as long as I didn't have to spend time alone. I hated being by myself. Memories would sneak in, thoughts flashed through my mind, tears welled in my eyes. With all the changes I'd made, the risks I'd taken, there was something missing.

My moment of truth would come nearly three years after I'd rejoined the human race. I think I'd known the answer for some time. Knowing the answer and having the courage to act on it are two entirely different things. What I lacked was spirituality. I'd taken my life back, had myself and circumstances under control, so why would I then turn around and give it up to some unseen entity? If I did, what if I didn't like what he had planned for me?

It had been suggested to me that if I wanted to be happy, turning my will and life over to a God of my understanding was the answer. When I could do that, there would be a clear understanding of where I fit into the plan. I would be given directions that would lead me to the life I was meant to live.

Frankly, I refused to believe that. However, a set of circumstances beyond my control brought me to my knees. I was so tired of being in control, of attempting to control everything and everyone around me, and still things happened, that I gave up. I surrendered out of exhaustion and desperation.

Such a feeling came over me. There was no burning bush, no booming voice, no ray of light through the window. It was just a feeling. I was not alone. I would never have to be alone again. No matter what happened, everything would be okay. The loneliness was gone, and I would never fear being alone again.

The initial prayer may have been made in desperation, but to continue that on a daily basis is an act of courage. To garner our faith and turn ourselves over to a God of our understanding and live our life accordingly, knowing the results of all our endeavors are out of our control, is courage. It's the courage to change, to follow the truth of who we are, no matter where life takes us, and continue to believe it is all for our best.

Today, I don't know loneliness. I embrace my alone time. I rise an hour earlier than necessary to be by myself, to have that quiet time when it is just me and God. I pray; I meditate; I think; I ponder; and I stay in touch with whatever changes need to take place in my life. When I am successful in my practice of these things, then it doesn't matter where I go, who I'm with, what I'm doing, or whatever happens outside me. There is a knowing it is part of the process.

God did have a plan for me. Part of the plan was to like myself, to respect myself, and through that to care about others—really care. I can't keep you from being lonely, any more than you could have kept me from it, but there is one who can. He will walk through your life, day by day, if he's invited, and you will never have to be alone again.

Fear of Love/Commitment

Love is the strongest emotion human beings experience. It can send us soaring to the top of the world and put us in a downward spiral to the pits of the Earth, and all stops along the way. It can be extreme, euphoric, mesmerizing, and painful.

We believe our parents love us because they have to love us, our children love us because they should love us, but it's entirely different when there is obvious choice involved. For some reason, that validates us more—when someone chooses to love us or to accept our love.

We love our parents, our relatives in one way, our children in another way, but to fall in love with a stranger is risky at best. And if we've been down that road before, lived through the loss of love, we know what it is to visit hell. While in this state, we begin to question ourselves. What's wrong with me? Am I unlovable? Unworthy? Did I love too much? Did I not love enough? Will I ever be able to love again? Is it worth the risk of getting hurt?

Fear of the emotional rollercoaster of love can driv
many of us to find substitutes. Sex is one. But love is an
emotion, and sex is a physical act. To confuse the two can
be disastrous. It took me many years to realize that sex can
be an act of love, but love is not sex.

Remember what it was like in the early years . . . those
first feelings of passion, the first tentative kiss, the brush
of a hand across the cheek? It's like a drug. Once discovered,
we seek out that feeling again and again. Even after we've
known the pain of love, we continue to search for it. It is
a most desirous drug.

Even when we become disillusioned, disappointed, have
suffered through love, and the fear sets in, there is something in us that continues to desire to love, to be loved.
We may tell ourselves, even act as though it isn't important, that it doesn't affect our lives, but that isn't so. As
much as humans need to eat and breath, without knowing
love, giving love, we are empty shells.

So, we find other substitutes. Pets are safe. They tend
to love us in spite of ourselves, unconditionally. All we
have to do is take care of their needs. You've heard sto-
ries of some older person dying, and when people enter
the house, they find eighty cats. That was a person who
had a great deal of love to give, needed to be loved, but
feared the love of people, the pain that investing so much
in another can cause.

standing in a group of people. One person tells an off-color joke that diminishes an ethnic group. We find it distasteful, but everyone else laughs. If we laugh, we give up a piece of our self-respect, our self-love. It may seem like a little thing, but it is that myriad of little things, those actions we take on a daily basis, that affects how we see ourselves.

What would it cost not to laugh, to walk away, to make a statement? It is fear of others not liking us, of not fitting in, that makes us go along with them. It has been my experience that some people may not like us, but *we* will like us, we will walk away with our self-respect intact. There were probably others in the group who were thinking the same thing, but lacked the courage to take a stand.

I believe God speaks to us from the deepest part of our being, from that person we really are. To know love of self is to act accordingly, to just do the next right thing. We must put aside our fear, what we imagine others might think, and our preconceived ideas, and listen to our God-self. When we can do that, we will know we are responsible for our own happiness. Nothing, or no one, can change the truth we live in. Only we have that power.

The same attitude change will carry us into a healthier, happier love life. The more we love ourselves, the more self-respect we have, the less prone we are to tolerate unacceptable behavior from others or ourselves. We will feel free to love, to be loved, in truth, and not because of changes we make to suit another or because we are living against who we really are.

We need to stop believing that what we look like, what we do for a living, what we wear, what type of car we drive, how much money we have has anything to do with who we are. Certainly, these things can be a reflection of who we are, but they are not the essence of the real self.

I got caught up in that. I tried it all. I became attracted, had relationships, got married for all the wrong reasons. I had this picture of what my prince would be like. I saw him tall, muscular, broad shoulders, thick hair, and a movie-star smile. I tried that. It didn't work. I tried marrying for respectability . . . someone who worked, was steady, had qualities I lacked. That didn't work. I married for money and security. That didn't work. I needed someone who was easygoing, with a great sense of humor, someone to have fun with. And still it didn't work. The one I didn't marry was the one man I was in love with, and had been for many years. I just knew if I did and it didn't work, I couldn't go on. So, love eluded me.

I spent fifteen years running from my feelings. I ran through affairs, marriages, the death of my one remaining child, addiction, a mental hospital, therapy, college, and through it all, this man, the one with the pale blue eyes that seemed to see into my very soul, lived in my mind. No matter where I was, who I was with, what I was doing, he was the first thing I thought of in the morning and the last thing I thought of at night. And he continued to be my greatest fear. He could hurt me, and I couldn't take any more pain.

When I finally got in recovery from my life, found a God of my understanding, I decided that was all I needed. I would live the remainder of my life alone, do the best I could with what I had left, and never put myself in a risky situation again. But there was still this man who lived in my mind. He called. I hung up. He attempted to see me. I resisted any contact. No one was ever going to hurt me again, because I wouldn't let them get that close.

In my desperation to resolve my dilemma, I finally prayed about it, turning it over to God. Suddenly, he stopped calling. I didn't hear from him for months. Three months passed, six months, nearly eight months, as I continued my road to self-discovery. I'd found some peace, even happiness. I had a job, some friends, was trying to live a decent life, had even learned to like myself. Yes, God had done for me what I could not do for myself.

One day, the telephone rang. I recognized the voice immediately. Something told me not to hang up. He invited me out for a cup of coffee. As I had learned to trust God in all matters, I agreed, and figured the least I would get out of it was some closure. As soon as I hung up, I asked God to show me the way, to let me know what to do.

He picked me up. We went to a small coffee shop, one of those where you have to get your coffee at the counter. When he pulled out his billfold to pay, there was my answer. It was a billfold my oldest son had made for him when he was in Cub Scouts, and there was a picture of my son inside.

For nearly eighteen years, I knew I was in love with this man, but had allowed my distrust of love, my fear of pain, keep me from him—keep me from taking the risk, living life to the fullest. He didn't meet the requirements of the man I thought I would fall in love with. He didn't look the way I imagined, dressed very casually, drove an old truck, and owned a bar. Considering I was in recovery from alcoholism, I didn't see that as a plus. But there he was, in my life.

We have been married for more than eighteen years now. Today, I know he is the most beautiful man on Earth. He is the love of my life. He is my best friend, my champion. He is my soul mate. Without hesitation, I can tell you that we belong together, and it is a love that will live on after we leave here. It was truly a God thing.

Later, after we were married, he told me a story about the billfold. It had been lost twice, once in a city 200 miles away, and had survived a fire. But somehow, it always came back to him. He still has it, still carries it with him. And each time I see it, it reminds me of the day I overcame my fear of love and how grateful I am.

People who have known us over the years say it was a shame we wasted all those years apart. Those years were necessary for me to find myself, to like myself, to ready myself for what was to come.

I had to find peace, happiness, on my own, in my own person, before I could have it with another. His love, no matter how great it was, could not give me what I was not ready to accept. The biggest commitments we can make are to ourselves and to a God of our understanding. When we can do that, we will know love.

Real love, whether it is of self or another is kind, patient, forgiving, and enduring. There is no question of commitment — it is simply there, a part of us. When we understand this commitment, this love, we no longer have any reason to hurt ourselves or anyone else.

Have you ever wondered if there is fated love? Do you question this "soul mate" concept? Do you wonder if God has a hand in bringing two people together? In truth, I believe it. Through my life experiences, I believe that when we stop trying to make our life happen, when we allow a God of our understanding to show us the way, that person, that very special person that we thought we had to seek out, will just be put in our path when the time is right. Trust in God and love of ourselves can overcome the greatest fear. Keep in mind that faith and fear cannot exist in the same moment.

Thank God, I found that one person who loved me, who cared if I fell off the face of the Earth, who made my life worth living. *It was me.* Through that discovery, I've discovered the ability to be loved by others. I can't tell you how many wonderful people have been brought into my life today, how deeply I love them, and they love me. The joy I feel through my friends and family makes me the wealthiest person on Earth.

When you are feeling unloved, perhaps unlovable, I hope you will think of me. Remember reading about a woman who, against all odds, found love. Realistically, if someone had told me the story of my life, I would have said you couldn't get here from where I started but here I am. Through self-discovery, faith, my fear has been replaced by a willingness to risk it all for love. It has been worth it. But remember what I said: When you come to this place, there is no going back.

Fear of Failure/Success

We all know what it means to fail. In the beginning, there's that big red F encircled on the top of our homework. It tells us we didn't measure up, didn't complete our task adequately. People who deem themselves as good parents will frown on this. There will be the inevitable lectures on "potential," on the need to try harder, even punishment for failing.

As we grow older, there will be sports, dances, parties, relationships to tell us whether we are a success or failure as a person. And it is devastating to a young person who fails to get a date for the prom, doesn't make the cut on the team, doesn't graduate with their class. These situations can make them feel as if they are different, not good enough, that they don't fit into the mold society has laid out.

As adults, we move into the realm of marriage, occupations, and parenting. Again, there are certain expectations that society puts out that tells us, in so many ways, whether we are a success or failure in all these areas. We may say we don't care about these things, don't think about it, don't worry over it, but it can have an underlying affect on our perception of who we are and what we do.

It was June 1947 when I came along, one year after the birth of my brother, whom I not so lovingly called "The Golden Boy." It's hard to follow perfection. He was clean, polite, and smart. It didn't take me long to figure out I couldn't compete with him. While he was getting straight A's in school, collecting awards for his big brain, I was sitting in the hall with gum on my nose, being dragged into the cloakroom for a spanking, and sitting nervously in the principle's office awaiting the arrival of my mother. I now know it is how I got the attention I so desperately desired.

By puberty, it was certain that my brother would be a success, and I would always be a mess, would always be a failure. They would just look at me and shake their heads. Believe me, if they'd had drugs for kids back then, I would have been put on them. Our life scripts were laid out, and they would lead me to fear success and my brother to fear failure.

When we believe we are not worthy, or we believe we must succeed over and over to be worthy, never failing, never disappointing others, it can be a great burden that causes unhappiness and stress.

I followed my life script for many years. I was Charlie Brown, always running toward something, and life was Lucy, always jerking the football away at the last minute. I ran and I ran, and I ran; and I kicked and kicked, and kicked, but never made the connection. I was the bad daughter, the disappointing student, the cheating wife, a child having children, and an irresponsible employee. I knew I was not worthy, and I set out over and over to prove it. To be the best at being bad, one must never allow good things into one's life. With success comes responsibility and expectations. Those were two of my greatest fears.

If I ever took responsibility for my life, for my choices, who would I have to blame for not making changes? If I kept my expectations of life low, I wouldn't be disappointed every time life jerked the football away. But somewhere deep in my being, there was a part of me that wanted a better life, longed to be a better person, who knew the truth of who I was. Fear of success kept that person locked inside me, just as the fear of failure kept others from being the people they truly were.

How do we change this perception of ourselves, of life? First, we must define what it is to be a success in life. There are those who have become great financial successes but are not happy. There are others who live quite modestly but have found true happiness. Which is the success?

That is dependent on what we believe. There are those who believe that this is it—we live, we die, it's over. For them, to acquire, to achieve, to attain personal power is the ultimate goal. You know, it's "the boy with the most toys wins" attitude. They will spend their lives in pursuit, but of what? In pursuit of success, in fear of failure.

There are others, like myself, who believe that there's more to this life. We believe there is a purpose to it all, there is a God of our understanding guiding our lives, and we are a part of the whole. When we come to believe this, our self-worth, how we see ourselves, immediately begins to change. However, it takes real courage to turn our lives over to some unseen force, to say, in essence, "Take me, I'm yours; do with me what you will." That's called true faith. And with true faith, there comes responsibility for our lives, our choices. The Blame Game is over. There are no excuses or justifications left. That's why it takes such great courage to do it for real.

Once the connection is made, and we start taking responsibility for our choices, our actions, we will know the meaning of success, will accept it as a gift. The successful person is one who is happy, joyous, and free, no matter their circumstances. I remember the first time I encountered that concept. I thought, *they obviously hadn't lived through my circumstances*. But another thought occurred to me: *I wasn't a happy, successful person before my circumstances tore into my life*. Since I reached that point, devastating things have happened, but I've changed my perception of them.

For thirty-five years, I failed at everything. I didn't finish high school because I was pregnant. I went through job after job, marriage after marriage, my children didn't survive, I moved from one dump to another, never had much money and few belongings, and was out of control to the point of addiction to anything that would numb the pain of facing every day. There were times I tried to straighten out my life. I went back to school and got an education, went to therapy, read all the self-help books, but I remained an unhappy, unsuccessful person. It was like there was something broken in me, and no matter what I did, it never healed.

Until one day when I accepted a God of my understanding into my life. From that moment on, things started changing. I believe, after that day, there were many angels sent into my life to help me, to teach me, to show me the way. Oh, things were wonderful. I awakened each morning with a song in my heart, filled with gratitude for every little thing I had. I still didn't have much, still lived in a dump, but it was okay. I had enough. And things continued to get better.

I married the man I'd been in love with for many years, moved into a beautiful house on a lake, had a car that worked, and always had enough to eat. It was like living in a dream. A few years later, I was given the opportunity to start my own business, doing what I loved. My dream to be a costume designer was realized. I worked hard and made a go of it. I knew life couldn't get any better than it was.

Just when the business was really on its feet, I was making good money, not having to work so hard, tragedy struck. I became ill . . . really sick. The doctors didn't know what was wrong. As the months dragged on, as I grew weaker and weaker, fear began to set in. I couldn't believe it was happening. For the first time in my life, I was happy; I was trying to live right; I had more than I ever dreamed possible. Why would this God give me all of it, just to jerk the football away again? I knew I was dying. I got angry.

A strange thing happened on the way to my deathbed. It was late one night. I went out on the upstairs deck to cool off. As I looked out over the still water, gazed at the clear night sky, filled with stars, a full moon casting light into the darkness, a feeling of peace came over me. I remembered someone I greatly admired said to me that if you believe one thing in your life happened for a reason, then you must believe there are reasons for everything. Faith is believing without understanding.

It was a moment of clarity. I knew that if I died that night, if I never saw another daybreak, I'd been given more than most. I'd known real love, felt unrestrained joy, a happiness I never imagined, was free, ready to fly, to go on with my life whichever way it went . . . on Earth, or in another place. Everything would be okay. The anger was gone, the questions were gone, replaced by an overwhelming feeling of peace and a knowing smile.

I was diagnosed with Graves disease. After treatment, I was looking at several years of recovery, many eye surgeries, and a lot of health problems . . . but I held onto that smile, that feeling. I wasn't alone. I was loved. Life was good even when I didn't feel good. Life was good even when I could no longer see to make costumes, could no longer run the business I'd worked so hard for. It would be okay.

My husband, the kindest, most caring human being I've ever known, asked me one day if I remembered saying I would like to write a book. It was pretty far-fetched, but when he came home with a used typewriter and a box of paper, I decided to give it a try. Today, as I look back, I realize everything that happened was part of the process, brought me to this moment in time, to the ability to put into words what happened to me, perhaps to touch another life as mine has been touched.

Today, I know I was not a failure. My life was a series of events that were a part of the human experience that prepared me to take my spiritual journey. Nothing is bad if we learn from it, if we can use it to help others, if we can see it as part of the process that takes us where we need to go. I am a success not because of what I've accomplished with my business, with my marriage, with my writing, but because I am happy with who I am, because I can still look into that night sky and know that wonderful feeling of peace, arise every morning with joy in my heart, and understand it's all good if you believe it is.

The only way to fail in this life is not to be willing to try something different, to open our minds to change. We are in a lifelong school, where opportunity after opportunity is placed in front of us. I believe that what we do here, the choices we make, will affect what happens when we leave here. And it's not necessarily the big, life-changing choices, but those seemingly little ones, made on a daily basis, that are so terribly important. Imagine if you knew, from the beginning, that there was nothing insignificant. What would you do differently?

When we fear good things in our lives, it's because we don't feel worthy, but if we were not worthy, we wouldn't be here. To be a success, we need to take part in our lives, to understand we have a choice in all things. The successful person lives with that knowing feeling—that no matter what life throws at them, it will be okay. The serenity that lives within cannot be touched by the outside world.

Fear of the Unknown

I've read that while we are in our spiritual body, or soul form, we have a choice to be born into this life, and that if we were completely aware of our subconscious mind, we would know everything that would happen to us right down to the way and time of our death. In this concept, we are here for a specific purpose, whether it be to pay back a karmic debt to another or further ourselves through the life lessons we need to complete. It's an interesting idea, and it would certainly explain a lot of things.

Imagine for a moment that this concept was true. What if, when we were thrust into this strange, new world, we came with that knowing. Perhaps they could attach a guarantee to us, like we get on a major appliance. It would state the required parts for the product, or body, to function, how to keep it fueled for optimum performance, and how many years it would last. Yes, there would be warnings, dos and don'ts to keep the product in peak running order. *Warning:* Do not insert foreign objects such as bullets or knives. Product will leak essential fluids.

I wonder how differently we would lead our lives if that were the case. If we knew we would only get twenty years, would we waste time on petty differences, on situations that wouldn't enhance our time here, on people who did not nurture and love us?

Of course, that is not the case. We pop out into an unknown land without a clue about what's going to happen from one moment to the next. We will be dealing with that for the rest of our lives. And we must remember that we are not the only ones dealing with that. It is a part of every human experience.

There are those who believe they are in control, can guide their destiny by sheer will and effort. When something out of their control happens, it can be devastating. One example was the great stock market crash in 1929. Many people made their plans, invested their money and lives in the market, only to see everything suddenly disappear. They threw themselves from the tops of buildings.

Others choose to believe they are safe from the unknown. They hide out in their lives, trying to stay out of the way of disasters, not taking chances. They tell themselves that if they live well, don't do bad things, bad things won't happen to them. But there is no place on Earth a person can truly hide from life.

Then there are the runners. They believe if they keep moving, not allowing themselves to get involved, not feeling, not stopping long enough to think about anything for any length of time, life cannot affect them. Believe me when I tell you that somewhere along the road, they will run squarely into life and the unknown circumstances that goes along with it.

How do we change the fear of the unknown into a belief that life is a fascinating adventure experienced one moment at a time? How do we find the courage to face the unknown circumstances that lurk in the darkness, in the secrets of life we are not privileged to? There are no guarantees, no instruction book to tell us how to act, to react, to all the situations we will be faced with.

Many will cling to the familiar, even if it's not particularly healthy, just because they know what to expect. This can apply to jobs, relationships, even a lifestyle. It's like going into a job because we need money to survive. The job may make us miserable, we may hate everything about what we are required to do, but we stay for fear of not finding another job, of going hungry, of watching our families suffer. Again, if we knew our time here was limited, would we do it? Wouldn't we be more willing to take the risks required, to face the unknown, than to live such an unhappy existence on a daily basis?

We marry or get involved in a committed relationship. It's fine for a while, but it begins to go downhill. We try to make it better, do all those things we are told to save the relationship. We have a lot of time and effort involved in the other person. For whatever reason, the person becomes abusive. To leave would mean starting over. What if we never find another person to live with? What if we can't make a living on our own? What if it's not any better out there than where we are? What if we get into a worse situation? These are the inevitable questions with no answers that plague our minds. Fear of the unknown can keep us stuck in a situation that is slowly killing our soul, day by day, minute by minute, as we continue to make excuses and find justifications for our inability to act in our own good. It's not easy. It's like stepping off a cliff into the dark oblivion.

Those who believe there is nothing more to life but this limited existence—that we live; we die, and they put us in the ground—wherever they are, however they think, will not change. To overcome fear of the unknown is to open ourselves to the belief there is something more . . . to us, to why we are here, to where we are going. Those who come to believe this, know they can step off the cliff into the unknown.

Life, for those who know they can fly, will give to them what they put into it. They open their eyes, their ears, their feelings, their souls, to every part of life, to every new experience. Life becomes an adventure, not colored by black and white answers, where things aren't necessarily good or bad, just what they are. They understand that the seem-ingly worst things in life can lead us to our best.

I always hated being poor as a child, not having those things that other children had, always believing my life would be better if I just had all those things I wanted. My brother and I would play army with locust shells we found along the river. We would line them up and throw clots of dirt for bombs. My paper dolls were made from cutting up old catalogs and magazines. We would build forts with blankets thrown over chairs and tables.

As a teenaged mother, I did some desperate things to make money so that my son and I didn't go hungry or with-out essentials. With no education to speak of, no real skills, I had to become adaptable to whatever situation presented itself. We survived, but we never had much. Pretty much everything in our lives was second hand, third hand, or worse . . . out of someone's rummage or trash. For special holidays, I made things out of whatever I could find. Once, when my son was in grade school, and they were having a costume contest, I made him a complete set of armor from cardboard boxes, tape, glue, and tin foil. He won first place.

For years, I had to dig deep into my imagination and teach myself to make things, because there was no money to buy them. There's no doubt life was a constant struggle, but through that struggle I learned what I was made of, that I could do whatever it took to survive. And I learned that I had a passion for taking some common, ugly thing and turning it into a fabulous, flamboyant costume that people would pay money for. Considering some of the jobs I'd had, that way of making money was like a dream come true.

Sadly, it was after my son was killed that I had the opportunity to make a living as a costume designer. When I did, I put myself into it fully and completely. Without so much as a sewing machine, and no education in the field, I realized my dream. I made fifteen rooms of costumes from old clothes, hats, jewelry—whatever I could find, and I had a very successful costume rental shop for many years. I won national awards and eventually wrote books on my methods of costume design.

Today, I know that being poor, as badly as I hated it, brought me some wonderful knowledge. It taught me how to survive on nearly nothing. It helped me realize what I was capable of. It forced me to use my imagination and learn to create.

There have been so many seemingly bad things that have brought me to this point in life. My alcoholism brought me to a God of my understanding, to a wonderful chosen family who is always there for me, always loves me, welcomes me. My pain through the loss of my children has taught me to treasure those people in my life that I love, to never take them for granted, and to know that every moment can be our last. Through a life-threatening illness,

I learned how fragile life can be and how blessed we are when we have good health. Unhealthy relationships have taught me to be what I want the other person to be in a relationship, that what I get is directly related to what I'm willing to give.

When I learned to step off the cliff and know that I fell into the arms of a God of my understanding, that was when I could fly. And I have been flying high ever since. It took everything it took, great courage to face the unknown in life, to step off that cliff time after time, but it was worth the risk.

I think life would be pretty dull if we knew ahead of time what would happen. I wonder, if that were so, what would be the point? It's all in how you look at it. For me, it is a great adventure, where I never know what will be around the next corner, over the next hill, down the next road. There is nothing really bad or good, simply one event after another that is part of the process called life.

You might ask how I can say a tragic event is not a bad thing. When we are in the middle of it, it's certainly hard to imagine it will be for the best or that there is a reason for anything that seems so awful at the time. That's why it takes courage to change our outlook. When we believe there is a season, and a reason, for all things, we can accept the unknown as a part of life. When we believe a part of us lives on, that there is more after this life, even death holds no fear.

We have a choice. We can take that big leap of faith, and fly, or we can stay grounded and stuck in fear of the unknown. Life can be like a rollercoaster ride. You can put your hands in the air and feel the exhilaration with the rise and fall, or you can duck your head and cling to the side waiting for it to end.

If today, your doctor told you there was a good chance you had only five years left to live, and nothing could be done for you, think of what you might do differently. Would you be kinder to those you love? Would you be working extra hours for those things you thought you couldn't live without? Would you try to fill each moment with wonderful memories? Would you smell flowers, taste food, make love as if it were the last chance you had? Would it open your eyes to the beauty of all you were going to miss, your ears to the subtle sounds of the world, your mind and soul to thoughts of a God of your understanding? The truth is, since we have no idea when we are leaving here, there's reason to live like that every day. And when we can live that way on a daily basis, we know what it to step off the cliff, trust in a God of our understanding, and truly fly. Fear of the unknown is gone.

Courage Means Facing the Truth

Courage is about the truth, facing it, and living in it to the best of our ability on a daily basis. The courage to change the things we can begins with the courage to admit that what we are thinking, what we believe, what we are doing isn't working. When we are not happy in our lives, have lost the passion for living, or live a fear-based life, perhaps it's time to reevaluate.

Remember what it was like to be a child? As children, we didn't overthink our choices. We climbed that tree just to see if we could. We swung out on a rope and dropped into the water, thrilled at the feeling of flying through the air. We jumped on a sled and threw ourselves down a snow-packed hill with no thought of what was at the bottom.

As we grew, those people important in our lives began to warn us, to instill doubts in our minds, taught us to worry. Society as a whole, in so many ways, told us what appropriate and inappropriate behavior was. They said, "This is right, and this is wrong; this is good and this is bad." Little by little, others' ideas seeped into our minds, taught us about fear.

Finally, we were grown, ready to begin our own lives. The ideas so aptly instilled in us by others travel into adulthood with us. We thought we knew better, things would be different for us, but the day comes when we open our mouth and hear our parents words and thoughts spew out. "If you climb that tree, you'll fall and kill yourself. You'll hurt yourself on that rope. What if you drown? That hill is not safe. Why don't you play in the yard with your sled? If everyone else jumped off a cliff, would you?"

Those are little examples, but it goes much deeper. The actions, the ideas of others, can affect what we think of ourselves, God, and the meaning of life . . . what is important, and what we are supposed to do to be accepted by the human tribe.

When we are unhappy, it's usually because there is conflict between the mind and the soul. The mind is giving us certain messages about what we "should" do, how we "ought" to act, what is "important," and the very essence of who we really are is telling us that's not what we want to do, to be, to cherish.

It takes great courage to listen to the soul, to accept the truth of who we are, and to change our behavior accordingly. How many times have we read books, seen movies, about that very thing? A young man raised among three generations of attorneys is expected to carry on the tradition. But his soul tells him he wants to be an artist. The family is disappointed, maybe enraged, and don't understand or accept his choice. He must deal with feelings of rejection, harsh judgment, being told he's failed them, the sense of not belonging, and the unknown. He must face the hard questions. Wouldn't it simply be easier to give in to please the family, to be accepted as part of them? What if he can't make it as an artist? Attorneys make really good money. What if they are right, being an attorney is a real job, not unsure and frivolous. . . . He would have security, other advantages, meet the right people. Art could be a hobby. His mind and soul are in conflict. What would you tell him to do?

What would you tell yourself to do? The idea that he'll do both isn't realistic. Usually when the choice of the mind is taken over the soul, it becomes a way of life. Ask people what they really wanted to do, to be, what their dream was. For many, it's quite different than what they are doing.

It is fear of being thought different, thinking outside the box, taking a stand on a personal truth that is not shared by the majority, that keeps us from change, from the very things we most desire in life. We want to be happy, but what are we willing to give up, to face, to achieve it?

The one thing we can change is ourselves. We begin by accepting the truth of who we are, and seek out those beliefs that work for us. Then, and only then, can we find the courage to live our life in truth, in happiness and peace, not affected by old messages, other people, and outside circumstances.

Think of the famous people throughout history who lived from the soul. The first person I thought of was Jesus. It doesn't matter if you believe he was the son of God or just an extraordinary man. His life, his words, had great impact on so many, for centuries. They are still with us today. He was the epitome of living from the soul, being true to his beliefs, living them every day in all things, even to the point of dying for them.

Jesus was a teacher. He taught through example, a man who truly walked his talk. He was a light in the darkness for those who sought what he had. What was that? He lived in truth, in love, in peace. He showed us that no matter the circumstances outside ourselves, we always have a choice. When we live from the soul, what can another person do to us? They can beat our bodies, abuse us in so many ways, even kill us, but they can't touch the essence of who we are . . . that part of us that will live on forever.

Jesus, and those inspired souls who have followed in his wake, through example, have shown us a way. Whether we choose to implement it into our lives is a personal choice. However we decide to live, when we have found the path to being happy, joyous, and free, we have solved the great mystery of life. What more can we aspire to?

Life is about self-discovery. The courage it will take to face the truth is nothing compared to the wonder of the life we will be given. I know this to be true, because I stand in awe of my life every day. I have known great cruelty, great loss, tremendous pain, physically and emotionally, but who I am lives on, is happy, joyous, and free. I have learned to live from the soul.

And Wisdom to Know
the Difference

LISTEN! DO YOU HEAR THEM? They are words of wisdom floating through the air, carried by the wind until they brush against our ears. We live in a world of instant communication. Through television, telephones, computers, newspapers, and books, we are flooded with information. The wise have learned to wade through the masses of information, discern the difference between knowledge and wisdom, and utilize it in their lives.

I've heard it said that if we want great wisdom, we must be patient and wait. Wisdom comes through age and experience. Frankly, I'm not sure we have enough time, or the stamina it will take to experience all things. Therefore, I believe it is a wise person who learns from the experiences of others. We don't have to set ourselves on fire to understand the pain, the agony of burns. We can see it in the horror of burn scars on another, by listening to their story. We can use the wisdom they impart to avoid the situation.

Life is like driving a car down the road. There will be bits of wisdom along the way, signs that tell us to stop, go, which way to turn, bumps ahead, construction detours, and other dangers. These were put in place by those who built the roads, those who had traveled them before. The wise pay attention. The unwise ignore the signs and believe there is a better way—their way.

I was the latter. I knew there had to be shortcuts, a faster way to get where I thought I was going. Every time I traveled that particular road, I ended up in the same ditch as before. And each time, the ditch got deeper and more difficult to get out of. I was unwise. I kept taking the same turn and was still surprised to land in the same ditch. Therefore, we who lack wisdom tend to repeat the same scenarios over and over, expecting different results.

Wisdom comes through paying attention, not only to the danger signs, but to the experiences of others and ourselves. My life was one disaster after another because I refused to pay attention. I can still hear the voices of my teachers, my parents, other relatives, imploring, demanding, suggesting firmly that I learn to pay attention. They warned me I wanted to grow up too fast. They told me to slow down, enjoy being a child. I didn't hear them. Grownups got to do all those wonderful things I was denied. I decided on the shortcut. That resulted in my becoming a parent at the tender age of fifteen. Someone had told me it only took once, but of course, I knew better. They were right.

When one expects to be treated as a grownup, they are expected to act like one. I wanted all the perks, but none of the responsibility. I soon found that raising a child was not like playing dolls. I couldn't just put him in the toy box and forget about him until the next time I wanted to play mommy. Working for a living, and to support my child, was not like going to school. Our very lives depended on my ability to show up and make money, no matter whether I felt like it or not. With no formal education to speak of, the jobs I had to take were not pleasant, not ones a person would be looking forward to doing on a daily basis. Surely, there was a shortcut.

I sold myself, my self-respect, for money, for food, for clothes, for jewelry, to feed my addictions. It seemed like the easier way to get my needs met, but in the long run, the price I paid for not wanting to struggle at a 9-to-5 job at minimum wage cost me dearly. But still, I didn't learn. Maybe I'd get married again, find a man who would support me. Another disaster lurking in the shadows.

I lived on the same merry-go-round for many years. I moved quickly from one job to another, moved frequently, in and out of relationships, marriages, and every time told myself it would be different this time. But it never was, because I kept taking my worst problem with me: me!

I could not benefit from the experiences of others because I didn't even learn through my own experiences. There were many who wandered in and out of my line of vision, who imparted to me those bits of wisdom they had learned through life experiences, but I didn't hear them. I wanted everything others had, those people I could see out there, but was not willing to do what it took to get it.

I was one of those sorry souls who had to lose everything and everyone before it dawned on me that I might be part of the problem . . . or all of it. The kids were dead. The last husband had long since given up on me. I didn't have a friend left in the world, and what family I had left wanted nothing to do with me. And who could blame them? I didn't even have a place to go or a car that would run. As much as I hate to admit it took all that for me to wise up, it did. I was at the end of my road. The merry-go-round came to a full stop.

Life is funny that way. We think we can run fast enough, far enough, that we never have to face the truth of who we are, what we've done, but the day comes when we meet ourselves on the road . . . head-on. It's like running into an enormous mirror. As we look into our own eyes, the truth will be reflected—the beginning of wisdom is to admit how little we really know.

When we get rid of all the clutter in the mind, the illusions, delusions we've lived with so long, it makes room for new concepts, different ways of looking at ourselves and the world around us. The mind is like an umbrella. It only functions well when it is open.

There was a poster I saw many years ago. It had a picture of a baby chick coming out of an egg. Beneath the picture it said, "What now?" I could relate to that. What does one do who has lived a certain way for thirty-five years, and then figures out it's over?

I needed help. I sought out a group of people who had built the roads, erected the warning signs through their life experiences and wisdom, and asked them to help me, to give me directions. I paid attention.

Through those people who had built a new road for themselves, I discovered the Serenity Prayer. It seemed so simple. All I had to do was find a God, accept the things I couldn't change, like my past and other people, have the courage to change the things I could . . . do better today, and acquire the wisdom to know the difference. I found the last line to be a bit tricky.

When we live life in the belief that we can force it to happen the way we choose, by sheer force of will, that we can manipulate and lie to others and ourselves, live in the delusion that we are different from the rest of the human race, always searching for the shortcuts, wisdom will elude us.

Wisdom lives in reality. Reality lives in truth. No matter how much we ignore the truth, doesn't make it any less true. The problem with saying the words out loud, admitting to ourselves there is a problem, is that once we do that, we then feel compelled to do something about it. But that is exactly what it takes to begin living life in reality.

What was, was. No matter how I tried to color it, lie about it, justify it, certain things happened in my life. The truth was that I'd been an addict, a whore, an inept mother, wife, person. I did horrible things, not only to others, but to myself. I was self-centered, selfish, jealous, and mean-spirited. I lied, cheated, stole, whatever it took to get my needs met, and justified it by saying I had to survive the life I was given.

What is, is. When I got in recovery from my life, I had to admit that everything I believed, told myself was true, wasn't. I had to face the fool that I'd become. I was wrong about just about everything. I was exactly where I was because I'd put myself there through my own choices, my actions. I'd had choices, and I still did. What I did with my life, from that day forward, was up to me. Life would give back to me what I was willing to put into it.

What will be, will be. No matter which road I choose to take, life does not stop happening. I can be the best person in the world, but there will still be illness, death, angry, unhappy people to deal with, work, chores, taxes. Those things that happen around me are not as important as how I deal with them, and myself, on a daily basis. I know I have reached a state of serenity when life is in chaos and I still feel that calm within.

How does one go about building that calm within, knowing serenity no matter what is going on outside you? That's where the wisdom to know the difference comes in. We can spend our life struggling against the outside forces, other people, but the truth is, the only thing we can really change is ourselves, the patterns of our lives, the roads we choose to travel.

When we are exhausted with life instead of exhilarated by it, when we see each new day as something to be tolerated rather than embraced, when we are sick and tired of being sick and tired, perhaps it is time for a reality check. We can change where we live, the people in our lives, make career changes, make more money, travel to new places, but what lives within will still be there. The same applies when we lose jobs, people, our home, money. What lives within can still be there.

I would like to share with you my guide to building the calm within. It's not really *my* guide. It is an accumulation of wisdom that I've learned not only from my experiences, but from so many who have so freely shared their experience, strength, and hope with me. They are the ones who helped me understand the wisdom to know the difference.

Stop

If we saw a stranger getting ready to step into danger, and we had the power to stop them, we would. If a friend or loved one was in great pain, unhappiness, and it was within our ability to help, we would do whatever it took to stop their pain. If we were driving along the road and a dog ran out in front of us, we would swerve to keep from hurting it, push on the brakes without a second thought about our own welfare. Why is it we will afford that kind of caring, kindness to a loved one, a stranger, even an animal, but not to ourselves?

The first step to finding the calm within is to stop and take a realistic look at our life. If it helps, we can imagine it's someone else's life and we have the ability to help that person. What are those things that are putting us in harm's way? What are those things that are keeping us in pain, making us unhappy? What can we do about them?

There's an exercise I'd like to share with you. Stop. Find a comfortable place to sit. Close your eyes. Imagine you are a superhero. Everyone loves a superhero. What special powers would you have? Most people would want to fly, to know the freedom of defying gravity. Okay, you can fly. How about X-ray vision, the ability to see through things? You've got it. Great strength? What would a superhero be without that? Super hearing, you say—that can be yours too. Now that you've established your powers, your task in life will be to fly around saving those in peril.

Now, what if I told you that all those powers are within your grasp? As a human being, we are endowed with great strength. In fact, at times we are amazed at what we can get through in life and survive. Every hurdle we overcome makes us stronger. X-ray vision is the ability to see through things to the truth of the situation. Try practicing in your mirror. What do you see? We have the ability to hear what we want, when we want. Listen—really listen. Clear your mind of those things you want to say, and hear the wisdom of the world through others who know. Believe me when I tell you that when you face the truth of who you are, become willing to change the patterns of your life to be a happier person, it will be as if a weight was lifted from you. You will feel as if you can fly. And your task will be to save someone: yourself. When you become your own super-hero, others will be drawn to you, will seek what you have.

The wisdom to know the difference between what we can change and can't is about understanding that we have great power over one thing, and that is our own life and choices. To tap into that power, we must first stop and face whatever it is that is keeping us powerless.

Connect

There are no new problems. From the beginning of man, it has always been the same. Oh, the faces have changed, the particulars, but the essence of our needs and wants has always been there. It's just a new take on an old problem.

When we think everyone is picking on us, that God and the world have singled us out, we overrate our importance.

I'm sure others, the world, God, has other things to think about than screwing up our day. Everyone has problems. No one, not the rich and famous, not the holy, not even presidents and kings can escape problems. So, no matter who we are, where we live, how much money we have, that is one thing we have in common.

Ah, you're probably thinking that a person who doesn't have enough to eat, a place of shelter, is much worse off than a king with great wealth. That is not necessarily so. Pain is relative and cannot be compared. Everyone's particular problem is just as important to them as the next person's, no matter their station in life.

I met a woman once who had everything in life I didn't. She had a beautiful home, designer clothes, some great jewelry, children, and didn't have to work for a living. I remember my thoughts as I heard her story of woe. It seemed her husband left her for another woman, someone much younger, and divorced her. So what's the big deal? I thought. I got divorced all the time. Good God, she ought to have some of my problems. My kids were dead, I wasn't sure where my next meal was coming from or where I would sleep that night.

Between sobs, her story continued. She'd fallen in love with her husband when she was no more than a teenager. He was the only man she ever loved. For thirty years, she invested her entire life in this man, in their home, raising their children. He was the only man she'd ever been with, or wanted to be with. He'd done well in life, had always looked after her and the children, took care of the bills, insurance, every little expense.

The husband was gone; he'd taken the money, leaving her in debt; she would have to sell the house, her things, to get out of the problem. She'd never had to work, to live on her own, to survive, and she didn't have any idea of where to start. The children would have to drop out of private school, the older one from college. How would they cope with going to public school for the first time in their lives? How would she be able to find a job at her age, with no real skills, and not so much as a high school education?

I got caught up in her story. I began to relate to the pain she felt. I wanted to help her. What was I thinking? I was barely surviving. The point is that her pain of loss was just as great as mine. We may have been from different worlds, but we were both human beings in pain. Pain is not greater, or less, because it is someone else's.

The second step to finding the calm within is to understand we are all part of one tribe. It is called "humanity." We are automatically members because we are born human. However, there are those who attempt to withdraw their membership. They are the ones who believe they are different and set out to prove it. I'm not just talking about the elitists who believe they are different, better, because they have great wealth and power, but the addict, people who attempt to take their own lives, commit crimes, who are in essence saying to the world, "My pain is greater than yours. I have an excuse to do whatever it is, to act the way I choose, because of my pain."

When we separate ourselves from our fellows, we walk alone. The solution to the problem is to focus on the similarities rather than looking for the differences. We have a choice to be a part of, or be apart from, the human race. Have you ever paid attention to what happens during a disaster? Suddenly, we are all in the same boat. It doesn't matter where we come from, the color of our skin, how much money we have, or don't have, what our profession is. We become simply human beings helping each other to survive. Isn't that what life should be?

Believe

Imagine that you knew for a fact that there was a God. What if you had a telephone, could actually hear his voice on the other end of the line? What would you talk about, tell him about yourself, ask about? When you hung up, how would you live your life differently?

For those who have found a God of their understanding, that is a reality. God is as real to them as the person standing next to them. They have a personal relationship with their God, can call on him anytime, day or night. He is their best friend with whom they can share every facet of their lives.

How does one go about achieving that type of relationship with God? To be honest, I had a lot of trouble buying into that idea. For most of my life I believed that if there was a God—and I wasn't at all convinced—that he was some big, mean, wrathful entity, just waiting for me to mess up so he could punish me. What I didn't understand was that it wasn't necessary for him to punish me. I was handling that quite well all by myself.

When problems arose, tragedy hit, I was in trouble, I tried prayer. I told him precisely what I expected him to do, but he never followed my directions. I look back now and see how presumptuous I was. I wasn't even getting through my own life with any dignity and grace, but thought I knew what he ought to do with the lives of others. And why should he be expected to get me out of trouble and situations I chose for myself?

It wasn't until I stopped, took stock of my life, and made the decision to join the human race that I could honestly become a spiritual seeker. To be a spiritual seeker, I would be required to let go of old ideas. To let go of old ideas was to give up excuses and justifications for living the way I did. What did I have to lose? Obviously, what I'd been doing wasn't working. My life was a mess, one drama after another, the idea of any calm within as foreign to me as if I were standing in the presence of an alien.

I set out to find a God of my understanding. I read books, listened to what others believed, and played mental gymnastics with all the different ideas. I was beginning to understand where others were, but I was still not sure how to get there. What I couldn't seem to get was the difference in *thinking* there is a God, and *believing.* It was suggested to me that I needed to move God from my head to my heart.

In a desperate moment, when I was on the verge of punishing myself again, allowing the excuses and justifications back into my life, I hit a crossroad. By then, I knew I had a choice. I fell to my knees, and for the first time in my life, I truly turned myself over to a God of my understanding. I came away from that experience not thinking, but believing.

What is it that happens when we find a God of our understanding and turn our life over to him? It's like going to that special place in our life, that place where we are safe, loved, free, where we never have to pretend, be, or feel anything false. We have made a connection to the source, to a love never before experienced. How do we keep that connection? We make it every day through prayer . . . through talking to our God. Through this great love that we feel, the warmth of the light that shines on our life daily, we will have a new understanding . . . a knowing that all is for our best.

How can we punish ourselves, do self-destructive things, hurt others, after we have become a part of something so wonderful? Our life will begin anew on that day, and it will forever be changed. When it is real, our actions, the way we think, believe, will be a reflection of it.

When someone tells me they believe in God, they know a God of their understanding, and in the next breath, tells me they are unhappy, I know it cannot be true. When people do things with malice in their heart, they do not know God. They may say, "Yes, there is a God," but that is the difference between thinking and believing.

I believe, through my own experience and the experiences of others, that there is a life we are meant to live. When we can give up control, surrender to our God, the path to that life will appear before us. Each step on the new path will be a leap of faith because we will know the end results are not up to us. But dear God, what a wondrous adventure we will be embarking on.

The calm within will stay with us on our journey because we know we are on the right path. Nothing outside ourselves has the power to shake that calm as long as we keep moving forward with a song in our heart and we know, no matter what happens, it's the way it should be. There is a season, and a reason, for all things, and we are not on a need-to-know basis. That's what faith is . . . knowing without understanding.

One day an atheist asked a believer to tell him to explain how he knew there was a God.

The believer said, "Do you eat salt?"

"Yes," the atheist replied, confused.

"Tell me what it tastes like."

He thought for a moment, then said, "Well, it's not sweet, and it's not sour. It has a taste all its own."

"You've told me what it's not. But what does it taste like?"

"I guess it's something you just have to experience."

"And that would be my point."

Reflect

Our past is a series of practice sessions. It's like learning to play the violin, kick a football, becoming a dancer, a skater, or whatever our goal is. Very few people get it right in the beginning. There will be false starts, mistakes, doubts may set in when we wonder if we will ever get the knack or it, but through hanging in there, learning from our mistakes, wanting to hear that beautiful music, see that football soar across the stadium, feel as if we are flying as we dance and skate, we will know it has been worth the effort.

For years, my secret dream was to be a costume designer. I had the gift of taking normal things, old clothes, and turning them into costumes. When I made the decision to pursue my dream, there were a few obstacles. I had no education in the field, nor the time and money to get one. I didn't know anything about sewing, except with a needle and thread, didn't know how to use a pattern, and didn't have a sewing machine. What I had was a wonderful imagination and a dream.

I opened my rental shop with more than a hundred costumes I'd made my way. People liked them. They paid money to use them. I stayed up at night sewing sequins and beads on, one at a time, and spent my days off making big heads from papier-mâché. Have you ever seen a weevil? I hadn't. But suddenly, they were everywhere inside the big heads—little bugs. I had no idea that by using flour to make my big heads, there was a danger of weevils hatching inside them. As I watched Rudolf, Frosty, Bessie the Cow, and nearly thirty others burn, I got angry, discouraged, was nearly ready to throw in the towel. But I was not ready to give up on my dream. I learned a better way to make the heads.

I joined the National Costumers Association. I would be attending my first convention. There would be a competition. I was so excited. I worked feverishly on my competition costume, the Queen of Siam. I sewed nearly 8,000 gold sequins on, one at a time. She would certainly be a winner. The night arrived. When I discovered there were only two costumes in my category, I knew it was in the bag. You can only imagine how devastated I was when I took second place. And the reason they said was that I'd sewn the sequins on by hand. Not an easy lesson, but certainly an unforgettable one. I went straight home and bought a machine.

It would be three years of attending conventions, losing, learning, and changing things until I won a competition. I can tell you, without hesitation, it was worth the effort.

Finally, my business was a success. Each year, my costumes improved, my clientele grew until I was shipping costumes to places like New York, even as far as London. My dream had come true. Suddenly, I didn't feel so good. Have you ever heard of Graves disease? I hadn't, but I had it. My energy level began to drop, my eyes were failing me, so I had to come up with new ways to make my costumes. Eventually, I could no longer run my shop, but I still wasn't ready to give up. They'd treated the Graves disease, but I was looking at several years of recovery and eye surgeries. What to do?

I had another secret dream. I wanted to write a book. My husband reminded me. I thought about it, and thought about what to write. What was it people needed to know about costuming? I considered those people—mothers, teachers, young people in theatre—who, like me, were not seamstresses but needed costumes. I wrote a book. It got rejected, and rejected, and rejected. I knew the idea was good. Maybe I hadn't delivered it well. I started all over, made new costumes, gave it a theme, and rewrote. It was accepted.

I started the second book. Suddenly, there was a problem. Something was wrong with me. My eyes hurt, my head hurt, I felt bad all the time. When the eye surgeon told me I would never be able to look at a computer screen without causing myself great pain, I was taken aback. It had taken a lot of effort to graduate from the typewriter to the computer. I'd just gotten the hang of it . . . and publishers wanted books on discs. But I wasn't ready to give up. I tried every imaginable thing to use the computer without pain. It didn't work. But I could still use a typewriter. It wouldn't be as easy, but it would work. And it has.

My life, like so many others, has been a process of learning, of changing, of adapting through my mistakes, my tragedies. As a young woman, I suffered great tragedies and didn't handle them well. But I survived, and I learned. Life became one practice session after another, and I got better with time. That's why, today, as I reflect on my past, I know none of it was wasted, none of it was for nothing, if it led me to this point.

We have a choice in how we perceive our past. It can be a yoke around our neck, holding us in place, unable to move forward, or as the school of life that teaches us so much. When we think about it, it wasn't the easy things, the things we didn't have to work for, the things we didn't have to overcome, that taught us. It was those seemingly bad things that got our attention, caused us to seek out a new way, to understand the need for change.

Through the loss of my children, I learned there was nothing else I could lose that would compare. The loss of a costume competition was nothing. Through overcoming my addictions, I figured out I could overcome almost anything. Even the pain of Graves disease couldn't compare to the physical and emotional pain of that. Through dealing with my mother's suicide, I learned to choose life. Death was way too permanent. Through all the pain in my life, I learned to ask a God of my understanding for help. Through this experience with God, I learned there is hope. Through hope, I learned about possibilities.

We may have to repeat some life lessons over and over before we learn, we may have to live through many experiences that we call "bad" to get our attention, to lead us where we need to be. The experiences themselves are not the point. How we handle them, what we learn from them, is. When we can look at life from that perspective, we stop looking at things as just good or bad and see them for what they are. Life is one event after another in a process of learning.

Remember what it was like to put on a pair of roller skates for the first time? I don't know about you, but I fell a lot, got a lot of bruises, ran into walls, at times got angry and discouraged, but I really wanted to learn to skate. So, I kept trying . . . practicing for the day when I would be able to glide across the floor. I wanted that feeling of accomplishment. For me, the past was the same. I tried new things. Some worked right away, others left me with a lot of bruises, angry, and discouraged. But I kept trying kept practicing life until I got it . . . that feeling of calm within.

When we talk about the wisdom to know the difference of what we can change and what we can't, we must consider the past. We can't change what happened, but we can change our perception of it.

I've thought about this a lot. If you looked at the details of the life I lived before, you might say that my life seemed cursed. I see my life as being blessed. I have been given opportunities to learn life lessons that many people will never know. It took every bit of the pain I've known to understand what true joy is. It took losing so much for me to embrace the gratitude I have today for everything, and everyone, in my life. It took failing over and over, at nearly everything, to know what it is to never take life for granted, to live to the fullest and stay in the moment.

Our past is a part of who we are, and to deny it is to deny ourselves. We've all had specific events, people, situations that have shaped our lives. Try looking back with an open mind. See what things happened that made you change, made a difference in your perspective, your outlook on life. Look at where you are, from where you started. Truth to tell, I didn't think anyone could get where I am, from where I started. I'm not talking about financially, the house I live in, the car I drive, my success in my chosen field, but about the person who lives within—the person who knows, no matter what, everything will be okay. Everything else is just perks.

Expand

When we say we can't, we most assuredly won't. When we want to do something and say we shouldn't, we have become slaves to the opinion of others. When we believe our life will never be any better, it probably won't. When we are confronted with a situation and tell ourselves going into it that it will be dreadful, it will. From the day we are born, we begin building our world from within. When we stop building our world, stop learning, we are stuck in the life, the beliefs we hold true at that moment.

To expand our way of looking at the world, others, ourselves, we must understand that what was true for us yesterday may not be true for us today. Just because something worked for us in the past, was true in that moment, doesn't mean it will be true forever. When we think that way, we live our life with limitations. For instance, if we've been eating fried foods all our life, love them because that's the way mother used to cook, then we are told we have an ulcer, it will be time to expand our thoughts on what we put into our mouth. Of course, we have a choice. We can continue the tried and true, stay with an old idea, and live in misery, or open ourselves to a new truth. That truth would be that if we continue doing what we have been doing, our body will revolt in unpleasant ways.

There's an old story about a researcher who was doing studies with children. He dressed two little boys in identical white outfits and put them in separate rooms. In each room was a chair, a shovel, and a large pile of dung. He waited for a period of time. He entered the first room to find one boy in the chair, as far away as he could get from the dung, holding his nose. When asked what he was doing, he informed the doctor that he couldn't stand the smell, was afraid of getting his clothes dirty, and wanted out of the room. When the doctor entered the other room, he observed the other boy, covered with dung, digging with all his might. When asked what he was doing, he said, "All this crap, there's got to be a pony in there somewhere." He had opened himself to the possibilities and was willing to do whatever it took to pursue them.

The wise will look at whatever their situation is and use the tools at hand to explore the possibilities. When we walk into a hardware store, there are shelves of tools to solve every imaginable problem. I believe we are endowed with every tool we will need to get through this life. But if during all our life we have used the same old hand saw to cut, and we refuse to even consider an electric skill saw, then we are stuck with what we have. Imagine, after all those years, getting an electric saw, using it for the first time, and realizing all the possibilities of what we could build with it. It will excite our imagination, our passion for building, and the same is true with our thoughts, emotions, faith.

Like a set of wrenches, each one designed to fit a different size bolt, we are given a set of emotions. There is compassion for those that are helpless, empathy for those who need understanding, anger to help fight injustice, sadness for those in pain, happiness for those who overcome, and love for mankind in general. However, like any tool, we must pick it up and use it. And the more we use it, the more skilled we become at using it. And it will take all our tools, practicing with them, discerning which to use for any specific situation, to help us build a life we want to live in.

One of the greatest tools, the one that needs to be used on a daily basis, is faith. It's like one of those all purpose tools that will fit any job, no matter how big or small. A person once told me that I shouldn't pray for silly things. It should only be used for big things, important things. I thought to myself, what is important to me may not be important to him. It might seem small, but to me, it was a big deal. What could it hurt to pray about whatever I needed to at the moment, as long as I understood the answer might be "No."

I use prayer and faith, my all purpose tool, in all my affairs. When fighting addiction, I asked the God of my understanding to keep me from putting anything nasty in my body each day. Early in my costuming business, when folks would call and ask me to make them a custom costume, I asked God to show me how. He was a great costumer. When I write a book, each day I ask for guidance, for the words to put on the paper. Prayer and faith are the tools that guide me through my life. They are like the compass that will show me which direction to take.

A while back, just as I completed a book, I came into conflict with what to write next. I've always had this dream of being a novelist, have written a couple of novels, but so far hadn't been able to sell them. I considered starting another one, but I was so torn. I prayed about it and held fast to the faith that I would be shown the way. Sure enough, there was a phone call. It would lead me in a totally different direction than I even imagined. With the new direction, I got excited, began to feel that passion build, and expanded my horizons. Perhaps one day I will be a novelist, but I can assure you it won't happen unless it's right, and in God's time, not mine. When and if the time comes, you can bet it won't happen if I believe I can't write a novel. Tools are great, but they must be used for the optimal results.

Building a life is much like building a house. No matter how beautiful the house, if we build it on sand, it will not endure. Faith will be the foundation we need, and learning to use the right tools, for the right job, will carry us through. We may have to go to others, to books, try experimenting with the new tools, until we find what works best for us. A great tragedy is to have the tools and do nothing.

With faith, with the willingness to do what it takes, sometimes digging through a pile of crap, anything is possible. One thing about it, if we are not willing to dig in, we'll never find that pony.

To expand is to open, make larger. The more wisdom we acquire, whether it comes from others, books, or experience, the more able we will become to deal with any problem. The more we can open our mind to new ideas, the larger our horizon appears. The bigger picture is always there, but where we view it from can be questionable. When we observe through fear and cynicism, we won't be able to see past our own nose. When we look at the world through faith, love, and optimism, it's like standing on the tallest mountain, where the horizon is never ending. But first, we must climb the mountain. To climb the mountain, we have to believe we can.

We have the choice to expand our horizons or stay where we are, stuck hanging onto ideas, old habits that no longer work. It's dependent on the willingness to use the tools we have to get where we want to be.

Live

We are alive simply because we are here. How we live is within our power to choose. We have the choice to exist, to go through the motions and get through the whole thing, or to live fully and completely, in awe of the gift God has given us, of the opportunities we experience on a daily basis.

Wisdom is the key to the difference in how we choose to live. It's a fact that for every action, there is a reaction. What if that were true not only for our deeds, but our thoughts, our emotions? I believe it is. When we live in negative thoughts and emotions, we may say we aren't hurting anyone but ourselves, but that's not true. The wise understand that those very thoughts and emotions affect our actions, affect those around us.

One of the most difficult things I've had to deal with is what I did to my son, Jon. He came into this world, a healthy, happy, beautiful baby in need of nurturing and guidance. It's true I was still a child—a child with no idea how to give him what he needed. I couldn't even give it to myself. The ripple affect from my grandparents to my parents, then to me, was passed on to him. There was no self-esteem, no self-respect, no peace in our lives.

Even as a young child, I can remember thinking I would never be like them, meaning my family. But I became them, and not the best part of them. And my son became me. Ultimately, that's what led to his death. Like me, he became an addict at a tender age. When he committed a crime, I worked out a deal for him to go into treatment instead of jail. He ran away from the treatment center. A short time later, he was dead.

You might say it wasn't my fault he died. He made his choices. But he was a boy. However, the effect of those around him, including myself, spoon-feeding him negative thoughts and emotions about the world taught him how to live, how to view the world. We may not have killed his body, but we most certainly didn't nurture or teach him the wisdom he would need to be happy, to respect himself, to know that life held other possibilities.

When the truth of my part in things hit me, I was sitting in a meeting. I began to cry uncontrollably. Some woman across the table patted my hand and tried to console me, but a man next to me told her to leave me alone, that I was probably experiencing the first honest emotion I'd had in years. A truly wise man. I understood, in that moment, the reality of what I'd done and not done. I accepted the fact that I'd been so caught up in my own pain, so self-centered, I couldn't even see what was going on with my own child, couldn't help him. Later, I would come to know that I was where I was at the time, and I did what I did because I had no idea how to do it any differently. I had no wisdom to pass on to him.

What does one do with a situation like that? There's nothing we can do to change the past. It's a fact. Certain things have occurred. We can stay in mourning, regret, shame, and guilt for the rest of our lives, punishing ourselves over and over, dwelling on the past and what might have been if things were different. Or we can take that experience, learn from it, and use it to grow and help others. I may not have been able to help my child, but through giving inspirational talks, working with other young people, perhaps I can help your child, or someone else's child. If what happened to me, to my son, saves one other life, it's worth all the effort.

One bit of wisdom I learned through experience is that it doesn't matter how low we have gone in life, how awful we may have been, we have something to give, even if it's only to tell others how not to live, what the end of the road is like. When we can use our past to help another, we will know it mattered, it wasn't all for nothing. We will no longer feel our life is useless and dwell in self-pity.

When we find a God of our understanding, allow him into our life, know that we are loved, we belong, only then, will we be able to love ourselves. The ripple effect will begin. Through the love of God, through the love of ourselves, we will reach out to the world with love, forgiveness, and kindness. We will be amazed at how many lives are touched by us. It's not that we have to set out to change anyone else, because we can't, but by living as an example of a person who lives happy and free, they will know there is hope.

Amazing things begin to happen when we live from the soul, truly experience serenity in our life. One by one, our fears will slip away. We will intuitively know how to handle situations, from the smallest problem, to the greatest tragedies. We will understand that with a God in our life, anything is possible. We are not alone. Our life has moved from "I" to "we," and every thought, feeling, and action affects not only us but the world around us.

Recently, I had a situation arise with a friend. This person became very angry with me. I wasn't doing what she wanted, the way she wanted, when she wanted me to do it. There was a phone call. In anger and rage, she put the blame on me for her problems, called me names. There was a time I would have argued, reacted with the same attitude she had. Instead, I let her say whatever she needed to, tried to hear past the anger to her pain, then told her I was sorry she felt that way. Before, I would have gotten very indignant and carried the anger inside until it was a huge resentment. The situation would have preyed on my mind, kept me awake at night, and convinced me that there was never any hope for the relationship.

Today, I know that everyone is entitled to their thoughts, feelings, and beliefs. Nothing I would have said to my friend would have made her feel any better. That is something she will have to come to on her own, when and if she is ready. If that doesn't happen, it doesn't have to affect my life, my serenity. I explored what she'd said to me and decided I'd done nothing to apologize for; therefore there was nothing to be done.

My life is a joy because I believe it's a joy. My moments are filled with love, laughter, and living life to the fullest. I stand in awe of my life on a daily basis and thank God for every minute I'm given. No matter the outside influences, my world is what I believe it to be at that moment. It's seven o'clock on a Saturday morning, the seventh of January 2004, and I am happy, at peace, and know if this is my last minute on Earth, it will have all been worth it. I have been truly blessed.

Wisdom Means Choosing How
to Handle Life's Situations

The wisdom to know the difference is about knowing how to handle the situations that arise in our lives to the best of our ability. We cannot change the past, but we can accept the reality of it and use it to be a better person today. We cannot change other people, but we can accept their right to be who they are, think and feel the way they do. That doesn't mean they have to be a part of our everyday life. Regardless of who is in our life, what has happened in the past, what our situation is today, we always have a choice, and if we choose, we are never alone.

In knowing we are not alone, that a God of our understanding can do for us what we cannot do for ourselves, as the fears slip away, the courage will come. We will no longer fear admitting we were wrong; we are sorry when we believe it to be so. We will stand by our convictions not fearing the censure, the judgment of others. When we live in the moment, we understand how precious life is, and we will not hold back our true feelings. We will not waste precious moments with anger, regret, guilt, revenge, and hate, but we will fill them with love, happiness, joy, and peace.

I came from a deep, dark hole, filled with pain and misery, anger and rage, into the light. It was a long crawl out, and I had to have a lot of help, but I finally saw the light of a new day. So, when circumstances arise, situations come up, I always ask myself, *Is this worth giving up my serenity over? Is this worth stepping back into that hole?* The answer is "No." There is nothing of this world that would make me want to go back in that hole.

If we believe life is some big competition with winners and losers, that accomplishments, status, and those things we accumulate have anything to do with how well we've lived our lives, wisdom has eluded us. It's about the person we are every day, in every way. It's about what we think, feel, believe, and how those things play out in our lives.

When we give with any agenda besides wanting to help, the giving means nothing. When we seek power over others, we give up the true power of our life. When we judge any person though ignorance or lack of experience in the same situation, the same judgment may be put on us. When life becomes black and white, according to our standards, we will live with the limitations.

Life will go on whether we decide to be an active participant or not. We have the choice to sit on the sidelines, clutch our fears to our chest, and watch life pass us by, or to walk through the fear, face the unknown, and know the true experience of what it is to live.

When we use our mistakes to improve our lives or the lives of others, we never fail. There is nothing we need do to prove we are worthy to be here. It's enough to believe a God of our understanding, believe it enough to allow us our life. The life we've been given can be viewed as a curse or a blessing, totally depending on our perception.

Each day we awaken to a new sunrise, we have a choice in all things. We can allow light from the sunrise to enter our heart and look forward to each new day with the anticipation of a child, or obscure the light with clouds of our own making. The truth is, when we allow anything outside ourselves to close off the light, we have no one to blame but ourselves.

It's okay to be happy, joyous, and free even when those around us aren't. People will come and go in our lives, situations will happen, life will be what it will be, but we don't have to let it affect us in negative ways. When we understand we cannot change others, that we have no control over events, the one thing left is ourselves. We will have to live with that person until the day we die, and beyond, so we better take good care of ourselves.

We are body, mind, and soul. Sooner or later, the body will fail us. The mind may play tricks on us, tell us things that are not true or are skewed in one way or another. But the soul, the essence of who we are, will never fail us. When we learn to live from the soul, we will know serenity, peace, and the connection we have to each other and our God.

When the connection is truly made, we know it in the deepest part of our being; doubts and fear will slip away. We will come to know that no matter what another person can do to us, we cannot be destroyed. It's simply a matter of being birthed into another existence. I believe the process is to be birthed through one tunnel to another, to live to the fullest in each existence, until we go home, return to the source.

What a wonderful adventure we have embarked on. Life itself, the challenges, the hurdles, the interesting people and experiences we get to share. I would say it doesn't get any better than this, but I don't know that to be true. But I'm sure the next existence will be another wondrous adventure.

If I could share one bit of wisdom with you, it would be to do whatever it takes to get enthused about life. If what you are doing isn't working, experiment until you find what does. Become an explorer, a seeker; open your mind to the possibilities.

Afterword

Am I glad I stuck around to finish out my life? You bet! I wouldn't have missed this for all the gold in the world. It has been quite a ride — and it still is, as I never know what is around the next bend, over the next hill, or will be put in my path.

I don't know who wrote the Serenity Prayer, those few lines that have had such impact on my life and the lives of so many others. I would bet, though, that they knew a God of their understanding who showed them the way. It is a wonderful guideline for those who want to find peace, happiness, a better way to live.

Through the Serenity Prayer, I have learned to live in certain ways. When a problem arises, I ask myself, What can I do about it today? If there is something to do, I do it immediately. If there is nothing, I let it go. Why would I waste one moment of my day in worry over something I cannot change? When other people, for whatever reason, decide they don't like me or don't want to be a part of my life, it's their right. What they think about me does not have to affect how I see myself, how I live my life.

When I'm wrong, I try to admit it and learn from it. Otherwise, I don't owe any explanations or justifications to any other person for my choices. And I have absolute choice in everything I do. There is no one to blame, no excuses left, for my unhappiness unless it is my unwillingness to allow it in my life.

I am a precious child of my God, and all that is required of me is that I do the best I can every day, not to compare my best with anyone else's, and that I live in truth of who I am and what I believe at that moment. When the secrets are gone, the pretending is over, we can accept the reality that is life. Only then will we know the meaning of serenity.

What I feel today makes all the pain, agony, and misery seem worthwhile. In my God-self, I know there is a reason for my being here. Perhaps it is to write this book, to touch another life, to give one other individual hope through my experiences. I don't know, but I know when I stay on my path, it will lead me where I'm supposed to be, with the people I'm supposed to encounter.

My message to others is that there is always hope, reasons for things that we might not see at the time. We have a choice in everything we do, and two of the most important choices we can make are to choose life and to choose a God of our understanding. When we can do that, and stay out of our own way, we will be shown the way to a most wondrous place that is difficult even to imagine.

So, if you want to ride over the rainbow like me, to a land called happy, joyous, and free, open your mind to the possibilities. Try something new, if it's only in one thing for one day. Find those things that work for you, and keep doing them each day. The time is now, because tomorrow may never come. Remember, each journey begins with one step.

When I sign off on this book, when I write "The End," it could be the last thing I do in this life, but it is not the end. I believe it is but another beginning, that who I am will live on forever. You may not see me, but I'll be there.

The Beginning

About the Author

BARB ROGERS LEARNED most of her life lessons through great pain and tragedy. After surviving abuse, the death of her children, addiction, and a life-threatening illness, she won her struggle to find a new way of life. She first became a professional costume designer and founded Broadway Bazaar Costumes. When an illness forced her to give up costume designing, Barb turned to writing. She is the author of two costuming books and three Just Try This books—*Feng Shui in a Day, Simply Happy Every Day, Pray for Today*, and *Clutter Junkie No More*. She is also the creator of *Mystic Glyphs: An Oracle Based on Native American Symbols*. Barb lives in Arizona with her husband and two dogs.

To Our Readers